"Suzie has not only written but lived these beautiful, powerful words. In our uncertain world, we all need to know how to hold on to our joy no matter what happens. Suzie is the wise friend and insightful guide who will show you."

—Holley Gerth, bestselling author, life coach,
and cohost of *More than Small Talk* podcast

"Each of us wrestles with sticky spots in our lives that try, on a daily basis, to steal the joy Jesus has promised for us. *JoyKeeper* helped me to identify a robber in my life. As I have put the truth I learned through *JoyKeeper* into practice, I have found a new joy I've never known. I now know that specific robber's identity and can send him packing when he comes into view."

—Lynn Cowell, author of *Make Your Move* and member
of Proverbs 31 Ministries speaking and writing teams

"For everyone who has ever thought joy was for other people (you know, those super-spiritual people who have the inside track to what God wants . . .), Suzie is here to tell you that joy, deep soul-satisfying joy, is available to all of us who love God in our own imperfect way."

—Kathi Lipp, bests   author

"Once again, Suzie cracks open our hearts, enablin
She takes us on an emotional healing journey th
we've never known. Her refreshing biblical insi
life. This message will lift you above your c   s
a word for our time!"

—Lorie Hartshorn, c   anada,
                                 speaker

"Some books fill your mind and others fill you.   *JoyKeeper* does both, and then goes a step further, guiding you through the process of knowing, keeping, and living joy in the midst of challenging circumstances. Suzie Eller shares honest struggles and hard-earned wisdom on every page, always pointing us to Scripture, always circling back to Jesus, the author and perfecter of our faith, who for the joy set before him endured the cross. And what a delight to find a thirty-day devotional included in the book, offering daily encouragement for all of us who want to embrace a JoyKeeper life. So well done, and so needed."

—Liz Curtis Higgs, author of *31 Proverbs to Light Your Path*

"Suzie's inspiring words serve as a reminder that joy is found in faith alone, and teaches how joy is possible during times of difficulty. She helps readers expose the hidden joy stealers in their lives, discover how to hold on to true joy even when life is hard, and uncover the beautiful story God is scripting between the pages of the hardships of life."

—Tracie Miles, director of COMPEL Training and speaker and author with Proverbs 31 Ministries

"A fresh wind of hope comes as you read Suzie Eller's newest book, *JoyKeeper*. Suzie grants her reader permission to be real about what we feel, while equipping us with the tools needed to leap into action as God's JoyKeepers. Say good-bye to worry and hello to deep, lasting joy!"

—Krissy Nelson, author, speaker, and TV host, Krissy Nelson Ministries

"In *JoyKeeper*, Suzie Eller shares words as encouraging and conversational as those coming from a dear friend across a coffee shop table. Suzie is a gifted storyteller, sharing biblical insights, personal stories, and practical wisdom. Each chapter is overflowing with raw transparency, healing truths, and scriptural hope. You—your soul—can't afford not to read her."

—Amy Kratzer, founder and CEO of Girl Set Free

"During family struggles, health challenges, and disappointment, joy can seem elusive. In *JoyKeeper*, Suzie Eller intimately shares her path to joy through cancer diagnoses and heartache. Using insightful reflection questions and engaging storytelling, Suzie invites every woman with scars on a journey to becoming a JoyKeeper."

—Dr. Saundra Dalton-Smith, author of *Sacred Rest: Recover Your Life, Renew Your Energy, Restore Your Sanity*

"I have watched Suzie maintain joy in the face of adversity. *Joy-Keeper* is written with vulnerability and profound insight, guiding readers to encounter joy in a way they haven't yet—by knowing. *JoyKeeper* is a lifeline when joy seems like a lost cause and a fleeting feeling."

—Jennifer Renee Watson, cohost of *More Than Small Talk* podcast and author of *Freedom! The Gutsy Pursuit of Breakthrough and the Life Beyond It*

"To learn and know joy that supersedes our circumstances is not only life-sustaining, but *life-giving*—to us and to everyone whose lives intersect with ours both now and in the future. This truth, this hope, has become the testimony of Suzie's life amid real struggle, and through this book she has chosen to become a kind and gentle mentor, a friend who is willing to teach us how we can choose joy in both the mountains and the valleys."

—Katie Westenberg, author of *I Choose Brave: Embracing Holy Courage and Understanding Godly Fear*

"Suzie's transparency, wisdom, and biblical teaching make you feel right at home and safe. I felt seen, understood, and mentored throughout this entire book. Not only does she offer powerful truths, she equips you with practical application for breakthrough. This book helped me rediscover the joy I've been longing for, and I'm forever grateful."

—Christy Rodriguez, speaker and writer, host of *The Brave Place Podcast with Christy Rodriguez,* and director and CEO of BraveGirlCommunity.com

JoyKeeper

JoyKeeper

6 truths
that change everything
you thought you
knew about
joy

Suzanne Eller

BETHANYHOUSE
a division of Baker Publishing Group
Minneapolis, Minnesota

Published by Bethany House Publishers
11400 Hampshire Avenue South
Bloomington, Minnesota 55438
www.bethanyhouse.com

Bethany House Publishers is a division of
Baker Publishing Group, Grand Rapids, Michigan

Printed in the United States of America

Library of Congress Cataloging-in-Publication Data

Library of Congress Cataloging-in-Publication Data
Names: Eller, T. Suzanne, author.
Title: JoyKeeper : 6 truths that change everything you thought you knew about joy / Suzanne Eller.
Other titles: Joy keeper : 6 truths that change everything you thought you knew about joy
Description: Minneapolis, Minnesota : Bethany House Publishers, [2020]
Identifiers: LCCN 2019056902 | ISBN 9780764235818 (trade paperback) | ISBN 9781493425037 (ebook)
Subjects: LCSH: Joy—Religious aspects—Christianity—Meditations. | Christian women—Religious life—Meditations.
Classification: LCC BV4647.J68 E435 2020 | DDC 248.4—dc23
LC record available at https://lccn.loc.gov/2019056902

Cover design by Emily Weigel

Author represented by The Fedd Agency, Inc.

20 21 22 23 24 25 26   7 6 5 4 3 2 1

In honor of
Vivienne Suzanne McDaniel
You brought incredible joy, sweet girl.
We miss you.

contents

introduction

When the topic of joy comes up, I understand that it can make us all feel a little apprehensive. It's confusing to be told that joy and happiness are the same thing, because the truth is that no one feels happy all the time. It's perplexing when someone implies that you are less than faith-filled because you're sad or frustrated or even angry. If you are reading this book, there's a strong chance that joy is something you not only want to understand but want to live.

Me too.

I am writing this book for the woman who has struggled to understand joy.

I'm writing it for the woman who longs for joy but doesn't always know what that looks like.

I'm writing it for the woman who is reaching for joy in a hard season. Joy is not only for you; it's yours to keep in all of those situations because of this powerful truth: *Joy is more than a feeling. It's a knowing.*

You see, if joy is reduced to merely a feeling, you'll be up or down according to your circumstances, and that's exhausting. You'll wonder where God is when people hurt your heart. You'll think that joy is beyond you when you make a mistake. If joy is merely a feeling, you don't enjoy being in the midst of a sweet season, but wring your hands and wait for the other shoe to drop.

I don't believe this is what God meant for any of us.

The early church was marked by joy. It identified them! Non-believers looked on in confusion as the church dealt with difficult people, everchanging conditions, grief and loss—but with a solid undercurrent of joy. These believers knew where to turn. They knew whose they were. They believed that God would show them the next step even when it wasn't clear. Even when it felt like it was all falling apart, they believed his will would triumph.

At the same time, they were oh-so-human.

They had to work through conflict. They dealt with devious and power-hungry people who tried to mess up every good thing they were building. They had to pray their way through cultural differences, differing personalities, and persecution. They experienced sadness, loss, exhilaration, excitement, apprehension, and all the emotions you and I wrestle with every day.

A JoyKeeper is someone who experiences real life. She feels all the feelings. She isn't afraid to be honest when things are hard. She's tethered to something bigger than her feelings. I know this because I wrote this book in an extended season of sorrow. As I lived out each day, I'd whisper this to myself as a reminder.

Joy is not a feeling, Suzie. It's a knowing.

That principle of joy held me close to the Source. It also reinforced six biblical truths that once changed the way I viewed joy.

I pray these same six truths will help you redefine joy as well.

I pray these truths will anchor you even as your heart hammers and your knees clang. We'll unpack them chapter by chapter. Let's begin by letting them tiptoe into your heart.

- God cares about how you feel.
- God is aware of who you are becoming.
- God is God, and you are not.

- God is your safe place.

- God's goodness is greater.

- God has a seat for you.

For some of you, these don't feel like truth right now, and that's okay.

We'll take them deeper together.

We'll make lots of room to work through each one until they settle into your soul like manna. Transformation will come as you and I honestly plunge into those areas where God wants to do a miracle.

JoyKeeper

Joy is more than a feeling. It's a knowing.

You are invited to live a life marked by joy.

Are you ready?

Suzie

part one

Knowing Joy

If joy is merely a feeling . . .
I will experience it only when things go my way.
I'll wonder if it's wrong to feel sad.
I'll be tempted to hide my emotions from others and even God.
Storms will shake not just my confidence, but also my faith.
I'll wonder why God gives it to some and not to others.

Because joy is a knowing . . .
I experience joy both in the ups and in the downs.
I am unafraid to ask God to meet me in my sadness.
I choose to live in transparency with others and with God.
I am grounded in my faith and my roots run deep.
I believe with my whole heart that joy is for me too.

one

give a sister permission to feel

I t was the year I call *scarred*.

The first scratch on my heart happened the day my daughter was diagnosed with cancer. Though I am a survivor myself, this was different. She is my daughter, and I couldn't fix it. For the next several months we walked with her and her young family through surgeries, doctor visits, and recovery. Some days I sat with her, just watching her face as she rested.

When we were told she was going to be okay, I took a deep breath. *Things will be better now.*

A few weeks later I went in for a routine dermatology checkup. The doctor pointed to a small freckle on my shoulder. It looked a little suspicious, he said. Just to be safe, he removed it and sent it for a biopsy. I was teaching at a conference in another state when I received the call.

It was melanoma.

A surgeon removed a four-inch chunk from my shoulder that next week. All I could think of while he was performing the procedure was all the places on my body where a four-inch reduction would have been more welcome. The surgery left a wide, uneven scar that took weeks to heal, but when the report came back the news was good. The margins were clear.

Once again, I am ready to move on.

I went back to the surgeon a couple of weeks later to have the forty-nine stitches in my shoulder removed. As he worked, he peered at my face. He grabbed a bright light and held it close. "There's something on your lip," he said.

Great.

More needles. Another biopsy. Another cancer diagnosis, which meant more surgery.

When I woke up from the anesthesia, I was handed a mirror. I gazed at the thick black stitches running from inside my mouth to my nose. I wondered if I'd ever look the same. Weeks later, however, all of my scars were healing. For a fleeting few days, I contemplated getting a tattoo to wind around the giant scar on my shoulder, just for fun. That didn't last long because I was so over needles.

"You've been through a lot," people would say.

They were right, but I couldn't help but be grateful. My daughter was healing and the outlook for her was positive. My scars were fading. Life no longer revolved around hospital waiting rooms or medical reports.

The year of scarred is surely coming to a close, and I am ready.

A couple of months later, friends sat around our kitchen table. Richard's cell rang, and he slipped away to answer it. He's a therapist and it's not unusual for him to receive a call at night. I was surprised, however, when he didn't return.

When our guests left, Richard trudged downstairs, his face haggard. He sat on the couch and patted a spot close to him.

"We have to talk, Suz."

The phone call was not from a client, but from our son. He called to share news that turned this mama's world upside down. He confessed he was battling a secret addiction. He was in a desperate place and had been for a long time.

We had no idea.

From the outside looking in, this seemed like an impossibility. He had created a start-up business that was a success. He traveled around the world, speaking and motivating others. He had a beautiful family and was surrounded by close-knit friends.

Looking back, it's easier to see the cracks, but it wasn't at the time.

We climbed into our car that night, both of us stunned. We prayed and wept as we drove. An hour later we pulled into a parking lot of a rural gas station halfway between our son's home and ours. As the glow of the sun crept toward the horizon, he told us a little more about his battle.

Afterward, Richard joined our son in his car and they traveled back to our home. I got into my car and drove to wrap my arms around my beautiful daughter-in-law and grandchildren. As I drove, I remember feeling that I had never felt so in the dark or clueless as a mom.

One day my son will share his story. I believe that with every fiber of my being, for God began a miracle that night. Our son continues to fight hard for himself, for his healing, and for his family. But I couldn't see that then, and the miracle didn't come overnight. We went through messy, difficult places as a family in those first few months. There were hard conversations. There were plenty of days when we weren't sure what the future held for our son. He unfolded his secrets over weeks, like a dam that had been cracked for a long time but now the rush of waters whooshed through freely. My emotions bungee-jumped. I was confused. I was sad. I was frustrated. At times I was furious.

Mostly I was numb.

One morning I fell to the carpet of my bedroom. I didn't have the words to pray. Until that moment, I hadn't given myself permission to fall apart. I was too busy doing what we, as women, normally do. I was listening. Trying to love the best I knew how. As long as I kept moving, I didn't have to deal with the thoughts that were always there, tumbling and clawing.

Lord, I don't know what to do.
Help my son and his family, please.
God, what just happened?

As I lay crumpled on the carpet, those feelings pounded like fists. I don't know if you've been in this place. Most of us arrive there at some point. Maybe you are there now. Psalm 23:4 refers to it as the darkest valley or even "the valley of the shadow of death."

It is in moments like these where joy feels impossible.

It is in moments like these we are most vulnerable.

Truth #1: God cares about how you feel.

. . . .

WHAT I FEEL: God is disappointed when I am sad.
WHAT I KNOW: God cares about how I feel.

Now is your time of grief, but I will see you again and you will rejoice, and no one will take away your joy.—John 16:22

. . . .

When we are in a season when joy seems elusive, a well-meaning person might say something like, "Have faith." While this often comes from a good place, what is implied is that we are lacking faith. So we switch to control mode. We create a plan. We put on a mask. We tell people we are doing fine

JOY STEALER

Trying to control things, only to feel even more out of control.

and fall apart in private. The more we try to control everything, the more out of control we feel.

This creates a cycle that none of God's daughters should ever experience.

We try to hide our feelings, but they are still there

↓

Which makes us worry that we aren't doing this "right"

↓

Which can cause us to distance ourselves from God,
when we need him the most

↓

Which makes us feel more out of control

What a crazy, unhealthy, nonredemptive cycle! Just reading this makes me want to weep.

As I lay on the carpet with my face mashed into the fibers, this is what I *knew* to be true: God saw his daughter, a woman with no answers and a hurting heart. I wasn't judged by him. He didn't see me as weak because I was sad and conflicted. He didn't ask me to pretend everything was okay.

Instead, I was incredibly loved and seen.

If you have ever found yourself lying on the carpet, your face mashed into the fibers, crying out to God, may I remind you of something? You are a courageous, much-loved child of God. You are in a challenging season, but that doesn't mean you aren't faith-filled. Your faith launched you out of bed this morning. You've looked to him for answers. Your heart is wide open for his direction. None of that is missed by God.

When we understand that God cares about our feelings, we are not required to control, hide, or mask those emotions. One description of joy that lights me up is this: We consciously walk into his love and care. This is what we do instead of hiding our feelings.

You may feel that God is disappointed with your emotions, but that conflicts with the character of God as demonstrated through his Son, Jesus.

What Does Jesus Do?

In John 16, Jesus warns that grief and sorrow are ahead. He had just told his disciples he was leaving. They are deeply troubled by this discussion. They huddle to discuss Jesus's words among themselves. He breaks into the huddle to assure them: "Now is your time of grief, but I will see you again and you will rejoice, and no one will take away your joy" (John 16:22).

Jesus doesn't get angry because of their uncertainty. He doesn't remind them of how strong they should be.

If we really want to get to know someone's character, we watch and listen. Consider these further interactions between Jesus and those who are struggling.

In John 8, Jesus meets a woman caught in adultery. *What does Jesus do?* He sees past her sin to her heart. He stands between her and the men ready to stone her. He shows her what real love looks like, then sends her on her way.

In Matthew 14, Peter takes a few miraculous steps on the water and then starts to sink like a cement block. *What does Jesus do?* He reminds Peter of who he is and reaches for him. He's not going to allow him to sink, not for a moment.

In Luke 23, a thief hangs beside Jesus and asks for mercy. *What does Jesus say?* He offers redemption. A thief leaves the confines of an earthly hell to walk cleansed and whole into heaven!

Stories like these, and multiple others, reveal the goodness of our Savior.

They also show us what to do.

When you are tempted to push down the feeling that you are sad, overwhelmed, frustrated, angry, or hurt, tell him everything.

Invite him to fight for you and with you.

Instead of trying to be something you are not, allow him to be who he is.

Feelings Are Powerful Indicators

Rather than being "wrong," your emotions are valuable indicators as you consciously walk into his love and care. When I was lying on the carpet in the year I call scarred, my emotions were telling me that I couldn't go a step further without his help.

I am done.

I was at the end of my own ability and wisdom. When I cried out to him, it was because I needed him. Not tomorrow. Not the next day. I needed him in the midst of that snot-nosed I-don't-know-what-to-do moment and all the days to follow.

> *JoyKeeper*
> Instead of trying to be something you are not, you allow him to be who he is.

Inviting God in to how we feel might not change the circumstances (or sometimes even how we feel at the time), but our God, who is mighty, all-knowing, and all-seeing joins in the battle. We may still be in a war, but God is on the front lines with us. This is where his goodness and character show up. We may feel overwhelmed at times. It may take longer than we want. Yet we are not alone in the battle.

As I look back at that year, I realize I sometimes felt like Peter. There were times I took a huge step of faith, only to sink like a rock. The water felt choppy. The winds were blowing. Yet Jesus was there to lift me up.

There were moments I identified with those in the crowd ready to stone the adulterous woman. I would hold a rock of condemnation, standing poised, ready to throw it at my own heart. In his goodness, God stood between me and that rock of condemnation, showing me what real love looks like.

Give yourself permission to feel, sweet sister.

That in itself will alter the course of the battle raging inside of you. When you are honest with God, it's a strong move. You name how you are feeling. You examine unresolved hurt or emotions in the presence of the Holy Spirit. You pay attention to how you feel instead of burying it (which only means it will erupt bigger somewhere else down the line). When we surrender control and are honest with how we feel, we partner with the Holy Spirit to teach us, redirect how we respond, and begin the process of healing.

Maybe you've been told that pushing down your feelings is strong.

It's not.

Perhaps you've believed that God is disappointed with you when you feel a certain way.

He's not. He's not. He's not.

Knowing that, how do we process those emotions with God?

A few weeks after my son told us about his addiction, I sat in a chair, my Bible and journal propped on my lap. The year of scarred was ongoing, but the Lord and I were talking about it daily. One day I wrote these words: *Is this my fault?*

I asked that because I often wrestled with thoughts like these:

If only I had been more aware.

If only I had prayed more for my son.

If only I had been a better mom . . .

When we ignore our biggest questions or thoughts—because they don't seem reasonable, because they express dismay with people or God, because they reveal our deepest insecurities—they don't go away.

They fester.

So I began to place those thoughts and questions and emotions before God in a journal. I named how I felt. I wrote down that burning question. I might not receive an answer right away, but asking it opened the door for clarity. The Lord could show me what I couldn't see on my own and plant a sprig of peace right where I needed it most. I didn't hold anything back, because he already knew it and loved me in the midst of it.

> **JOY STEALER**
> Hiding your feelings from God when he already knows and loves you like crazy.

I want to invite you to do the same. As you pause to do this simple exercise, ask God to join you from the very beginning. Share the emotion you are experiencing right now. Write down that burning question. Then pray about it with a God who loves you right where you are. I've shared the beginning of a prayer to get you started.

JoyKeeper

When you are honest with God, you give yourself permission to feel (and heal).

PAUSE POINT

I feel . . .

_____

_____

_____

Jesus, the burning question that won't go away is . . .

_____

_____

_____

#prayerstarter

> *Lord, thank you that you are near. I don't have to hide from you or pretend that I feel a certain way when I don't. You know me better than anyone. You know my heart. . . . [Finish this prayer in your own words. Remember he loves you so much.]*

Once you finish this exercise, you may experience new and different emotions, and that's okay.

In fact, it's normal.

The Holy Spirit leads into *all* truth (John 16:13). Not partial truth. Not your next-door neighbor's truth. Not even your pastor's truth. *All* truth. When we are honest about how we feel in his presence, our eyes are opened to see the beauty of God at work right where we are. We may also see an area he wants to work in or shift in a new direction. If there's anything that makes you feel inadequacy or shame or embarrassment, then do the exercise again.

Do this as many times as you need.

If you feel a sense of relief or peace, thank him. He's rejoicing with you.

Perhaps you are reading this and life is good. You wonder if an exercise like this is for you. It is! This type of conversation between you and Jesus is not just for the harder days. When you talk to him about how you feel on a regular basis, conversation transitions to intimacy. That becomes a norm in your relationship with him. Intimacy removes hurdles that keep you stuck and offers a sacred place to share your happiness, excitement, and thoughts. When you hit the next hard situation, you run to him because it's natural. It's part of your relationship.

The more we make room to share our feelings with Jesus, the less they need their own room on the inside of us.

A Twist: Joy *and* Sorrow

Let's go back to John 16. If you remember, Jesus is warning his friends that grief is ahead. But he also says something surprising: "Very truly I tell you, you will weep and mourn while the world rejoices. You will grieve, but your grief will turn to joy" (John 16:20).

Over the next few days, Jesus's words come to life. Someone in their inner circle betrays Jesus, leading a group of soldiers under the cover of darkness to arrest Jesus. They experience sorrow that comes through unfaithfulness and betrayal.

When they resist the soldiers, pulling out their swords, they are instructed by Jesus to step back. Oh, the pain that comes as they feel the sorrow of helplessness.

Later, they stand in the crowd as an unjust court accuses Jesus and a guilty man is released in his place. Injustice might feel like the greatest sorrow.

Sorrow upon sorrow, it keeps coming.

> *JoyKeeper*
> The more you make room to share your feelings with Jesus, the less they need their own room inside you.

Jesus lays down on a rugged cross. He dies. They are shattered. *Oh, the sorrow of losing someone you love.*

They mourned, just as Jesus said they would . . . but didn't he say something about joy?

Is it possible to know joy in a time such as this?

> You will grieve, but your grief will turn to joy. A woman giving birth to a child has pain because her time has come; but when her baby is born she forgets the anguish because of her joy that a child is born into the world.—John 16:20–21

When I think about words associated with pregnancy and birth, these rise to the top: *expectation, waiting, fear of the unknown, labor, pain, apprehension, excitement, joy.*

When my oldest, Leslie, was only ten months old, I stood in the bathroom with my hands on my stomach. I was pregnant and my oldest wasn't walking yet. I was still nursing. She had another year in diapers. I wanted a big family, but this wasn't my plan. A few weeks later I found out I was carrying twins. To the woman who longs to hold her child and it hasn't happened, this sounds selfish, but this was what was going on in my heart. When Leslie was born, I wasn't sure how to be a mom. There was a learning curve, and it felt overwhelming. I loved her with all my heart and was step-by-step figuring out this thing called parenting. But this unexpected news seemed really big. Having three children under the age of nineteen months seemed like an impossible gift.

It was like training for a 5K and crossing the finish line with a passable time, only to find out you are now scheduled to run a full marathon the next week. I wrestled with all of the feelings—exhilaration, excitement, apprehension, happiness, fear, fear, and more fear.

A few months later the doctor placed Melissa in my arms. Three minutes later he placed Ryan beside her. Melissa blinked up at me with blue-green eyes. She was petite and beautiful. Her brother was all arms and legs. When they placed him next to his sister, he studied my face. He had deep brown eyes like my mother's. Richard brought Leslie in. She was nineteen months old, barely a toddler. She perched on the edge of the hospital bed, fascinated by the two human beings in my arms.

Something transitioned in that moment.

I had no doubt it was going to be hard. There was a mountain of diapers, spit-up, sleepless nights, and tears ahead.

But these were my people.

We'd figure it out. I'd grow as a mom. I'd learn. I'd read a ton of books and pray and ask for help where I could find it. My plans were going out the window and I didn't think for one minute that it would be easy, but that was okay because Richard and I were now a family of five, and it was beautiful. In the midst of my uncertainty and labor and apprehension and fear, God was birthing a story. Not just my story, but also the story of those tiny human beings.

Perhaps that is why Jesus likened joy to childbirth.

God's plan isn't to replace sorrow with joy, but to write a new story of joy through sorrow. That's what he did with the early church. Jesus suffered. He died on the cross. They were afraid. They suffered persecution.

All of these things brought sorrow, but joy was birthed through that sorrow. We see this same pattern all through Scripture.

A story of sorrow	*A story of joy*
Jesus suffered on the cross.	Through sorrow the stronghold of sin was conquered.
Jesus left his disciples to return to heaven.	Through sorrow they were launched into purpose and became the church.
Persecution felt like . . . well, persecution.	Sorrow scattered them farther than they'd ever been before. As a result, their message spread wide, reaching more people than imagined possible.

Sorrow *and* joy. Waltzing together in heavenly cadence.

Sorrow and joy changed Jesus's followers. It changed the way they viewed their faith. Sorrow and joy even changed the way they viewed Jesus. When Jesus and his followers lived in close proximity, they witnessed him as he performed miracles. Jesus's name had always meant something to them—rabbi, teacher, friend.

After the cross and resurrection, his name took on greater significance. It wasn't just that of a great teacher or a good friend, it was the name of the risen Messiah! Joy burst through sorrow as new stories were written in the name of Jesus. They laid hands on the sick, shared the gospel with the lost, and saw the demonized released from their torment—*in* his name.

Just as joy was a mark of the early church, it's also a mark of our faith.

As time passed, I started to see the beauty of what God was doing in the year I called scarred. At first it, was like peering through a crystal window, but now I see it more clearly. When I look back at my journals, I see sorrow splashed on the pages. With hindsight, I also see glimpses of the joy being written.

One day, years from now, I will look back and see the deeper reality of God's goodness in those hard places.

31

Real Life

When I was younger, I shared a problem with an older woman. The details were private. She didn't have any answers, but she listened and I left feeling better.

"Please don't tell anyone" were my last words in our conversation.

The next day I received a phone call. A woman I didn't know well described my problem in vivid detail and then offered advice. I was so stunned I nearly dropped the phone.

When I pulled myself together, I asked how she knew. She said the woman I had talked with the day before had called her. I later discovered the older woman had made several calls moments after I left her home.

When I confronted her gently, the surprise on her face was genuine.

"I just wanted to help," she said.

Most people are not cruel. They aren't trying to make you feel bad or pile hurt on top of already-bruised feelings. They don't want to give you bad advice or betray your trust. But can we be honest? Sometimes the worst advice we receive comes from a place of caring. The other person doesn't know what to say, or thinks she understands what is going on.

We receive it. We listen. Then we walk away feeling ten times more burdened. We may try to explain, but it gets more muddled. I learned a lesson that day. This was someone I would care for as a friend, but I wouldn't go to her as a confidante.

Sharing your feelings is strong, but knowing where to share them is essential.

Talking through your feelings with God is the safest place to begin. A conversation with God may lead you to a godly friend or counselor to help you continue to sort through your feelings.

The whole world doesn't get access. This is not for social media. It's not for that person who advises you to go the opposite of your faith. If anyone makes you feel ashamed of how you feel, then it's probably an area where God is still working in that person and you keep going. You aren't required to receive any unhelpful or damaging gift of advice. If someone offers a five-step plan that helped her, but it doesn't help you, that doesn't make you a failure. It just means that you are two different people in two different circumstances.

When you share how you feel first with Jesus, you bring it to the One who sees the whole picture. He understands your motivations, where you need help or rest or assurance, as well as those areas where you might need to grow, change direction, wait, or trust.

Knowing whom to trust isn't always easy, but you can trust that he cares about how you feel.

Joy Keeper:
Give Yourself Permission to Feel

· ·

Truth

It's obvious, of course, that he didn't go to all this trouble for angels. It was for people like us, children of Abraham. That's why he had to enter into every detail of human life. Then, when he came before God as high priest to get rid of the people's sins, he would have already experienced it all himself—all the pain, all the testing—and would be able to help where help was needed.—Hebrews 2:16–19 MESSAGE

Live It

- Acknowledge how you feel.
- Share it with Jesus first.

Start a habit of talking to Jesus daily. I set a timer for eleven minutes each morning. For the prayer warrior who prays for hours, that might not seem like much. For the distracted in-love-with-Jesus woman like me, it makes perfect sense. It's become the best part of my day. That eleven minutes can seem like a really long time on days when I am hurting or my words don't come easy, but there is still a beautiful work that takes place because I choose to be present. At other times, the minutes fly and I turn off the timer, and we just keep talking.

Jesus, I choose to honestly share how I feel with you, rather than pretend. You see what I do not. You are with me in the good and also harder seasons. I hold up my feelings, that circumstance, or that person on my heart and invite you in. Amen.

two

becoming

I was at a large gathering of friends and had just wrestled with a tired, overstimulated toddler who tried to stab me in the eye with a fork. A friend came up behind me and said something teasing. Something like, "What did you do to that baby?"

You've been there, right?

You are doing all you know to do and it's not working and it's on public display. Then someone says something, and it hits a way-too-tender spot. I think I smiled even as she continued to tease. She wasn't trying to be unkind. It was just bad timing.

I replied with, "Um, I'm not doing anything to this baby." My slightly on-edge tone should have been a signal to me that an insignificant moment was about to take up significant emotional bandwidth.

It's exactly insignificant moments like these that can turn into arguments, division, and hurt feelings—and even last years after the moment is forgotten by everyone else. Something little sparks something big in us and suddenly it's Armageddon. If not externally with another person, the war is raging inside.

It is important for us to know ourselves in those moments.

I'm an introvert, and this was day four of parties and travel and close-knit interaction. I was grateful, but I was also about two days overdue for an alone-time fill-up. I was just as overstimulated as the little guy with the fork. It was time to pull away, find a quieter spot, and take a deep breath.

Years ago, it didn't quite work this way. I struggled with a canyon-sized crack in my heart. I battled against my tendency to take things personally. If my child was cranky, my go-to was to mentally list what I had done for him or her that day, rather than see that my child was two and needed a nap (and mama needed one too). If conflict arose, I either ran the other way or allowed it to hurt my heart, rather than work through it. I never stopped to consider where it was coming from or why it was taking place. The battle was a solitary one. Most people didn't know this about me because the skirmish was going on inside of me.

While I don't like sharing that with you, I'm not revealing it to beat myself up. This was simply an area of my heart that needed healing. When God heals any wound, temptation creeps back in from time to time. That's what happened the night a friend teased me. There's a quote that I love—there's so much wisdom in it:

> An unhealed person can find offense in pretty much anything anyone does. A healed person understands the actions of others have nothing to do with them. Each day you get to decide which you will be.—Unknown

I had a lot of options available to me:

- I could take the light-hearted teasing personally.
- I could blow it up bigger than it should be.
- I could respond as a healed woman.

Which would I choose?

Truth #2:
God knows who you are becoming.

. . . .

WHAT I FEEL: I will never be enough.
WHAT I KNOW: God is aware of who I am becoming.

He knows us far better than we know ourselves, knows our pregnant condition, and keeps us present before God. That's why we
can be so sure that every detail in our lives of love for God is
worked into something good. God knew what he was doing from
the very beginning.—Romans 8:27–29 MESSAGE

. . . .

One of the most damaging joy stealers is feeling like we will never
measure up.

That often transitions into placing impossible standards on our
relationship with God. Imagine that you meet someone special,
but from the beginning you place unreasonable expectations on
the relationship. The expectations aren't on the other person, they
are on you. They might look something like this:

- You have to be perfect to earn the other's love.
- You can never make a mistake. If you do, you expect pun-
  ishment or even abandonment.
- You are constantly striving, working, and perfecting yourself because otherwise you'll never measure up.
- You keep count of wrongs. Not just your own, but those
  of others.

These are [wo]manmade barriers that keep us at a distance in
our relationship with God.

The danger is that when we fall short, we may give up.

These joy stealers are traps set by an enemy who wants nothing more than to disrupt the power of intimacy between Jesus and those he loves.

The Power of Knowing Jesus

If I look at a list of women born in the 1990s, about half of the names seem to start with either a J or a K. That's how it was with the name Mary in biblical times. If you were to walk down the streets of a typical Jewish city, nearly a quarter of women would be called Mariam, Maryam, or Miriam (the Hebrew and Greek versions of Mary).

Two of the women closest to Jesus were named Mary. One a young innocent virgin. The other a woman tormented by demonic influence. Though the name they shared could be described as common, each had a relationship with Jesus that was extraordinary.

Mary the mother of Jesus met him the day she held him in her arms for the first time. Though he was wrinkled and appeared like any other infant, she knew he was special. His conception holy. His purpose beyond comprehension for this young woman.

She had no idea what to expect as the mother of Jesus. She had no idea how living in close proximity to this child would change her.

Mary Magdalene was a friend of Jesus. She was distinguished from other Marys by the city she was associated with. She came from Magdala, a town located on the north shore of Galilee. We first meet Mary as she and a group of other grateful women follow Jesus from place to place:

> JOY STEALER
> Setting impossible standards in your relationship with God and with others.

After this, Jesus traveled about from one town and village to another, proclaiming the good news of the kingdom of God. The

Twelve were with him, and also some women who had been cured of evil spirits and diseases: Mary (called Magdalene) from whom seven demons had come out; Joanna the wife of Chuza, the manager of Herod's household; Susanna; and many others. These women were helping to support them out of their own means.—Luke 8:1–3

There are times when I read a story that I want all the details. This is one of them. I long to know how old Mary Magdalene was. She seems older because she had the ability to contribute financially. I want to know if she was an outcast and how her torment affected her relationship with her family. I wish I could have stood in the crowd as she approached Jesus, or perhaps been a fly on the wall as he recognized her pain for the first time. I can almost see him placing his hands on her face, like he did the blind man, and speaking peace over her anguish.

Scripture doesn't tell us the complete story, as much as we want to hear it. What we do know is that her encounter with Jesus freed her from seven demons. This once distressed, tortured woman believed in his message so much that she shadowed him wherever he went and supported his mission to love the world.

Relationships alter us—especially with those closest to us.

What closer relationship can we have than that with our Savior?

Mary the mother of Jesus matured from a young girl to a mother of a grown man. Jesus often confounded her, speaking of his Father's wishes when all she wanted was for him to listen to her. At the age of twelve, he and his family went to Jerusalem. When it was time to leave, Mary and her family traveled with a crowd toward home. At some point in the journey, she noticed Jesus was missing.

It took three days to find him. *Three days!*

When Mary finally located him, Jesus was casually standing in front of a crowd older and more distinguished than a mere twelve-year-old boy. Jesus was teaching them, not worried at all about the fact that his mom was scared out of her mind.

When his parents saw him, they were astonished. His mother said to him, "Son, why have you treated us like this? Your father and I have been anxiously searching for you."

"Why were you searching for me?" he asked. "Didn't you know I had to be in my Father's house?" But they did not understand what he was saying to them.—Luke 2:48–50

Mary often asserted herself as Jesus's mama. Sometimes it went well, other times it didn't. She once asked Jesus to turn water into wine at a wedding. When Jesus said it wasn't his time, she asked him to perform the miracle anyway. Jesus consented. This makes me smile.

Jesus is King of Kings, but Mama pulled rank.

Another time Mary heard about the long hours Jesus spent praying for people and teaching. The report came back to his family that he was exhausted. Mary was more than willing to tell her thirty-year-old son what she thought about that. So she grabbed her other children and made her way to him.

Then Jesus entered a house, and again a crowd gathered, so that he and his disciples were not even able to eat. When his family heard about this, they went to take charge of him, for they said, "He is out of his mind."—Mark 3:20–21

Mary and her sons knocked on the door and sent a message summoning Jesus. He didn't come. He continued right on ministering. Can you imagine how Mary felt? Conflicted. Frustrated. The mother in her wrestled with the understanding that Jesus was the Messiah.

Though their stories are different, one of the most powerful images of the two Marys is portrayed on the day Jesus suffered and died.

Both at the foot of the cross.

Most of his followers had fled or hidden away, as at that time it was dangerous to be an ally of Jesus. Yet here they were. Mary the mama and Mary Magdalene. For one, the unimaginable had just taken place. Her son dangled from a brutal cross, a crown of thorns piercing his brow. For the other, her Savior and rescuer was experiencing the worst moment of his earthly existence. Both were present. Not only at his death, but also at his burial, and later his resurrection. The fact that these two women knelt courageously by his side tells us they were radically changed because of their relationship with him. Mary the mother of Jesus is no longer a frightened, innocent girl. She's a lioness of a mother, standing against the world to remain near to her son. Mary Magdalene is no longer a victim. She's a warrior. Jesus met her in her worst hour, and now, regardless of danger, she will stay close to him.

We have no idea how our relationship with Jesus will transform us. We have no idea where it will lead, or the strength it will produce. But Jesus knows. Yes, he does.

The Power of Being Known by Jesus

I'm forty years into my relationship with Jesus. I love him and can't imagine life without my faith. I've grown in a thousand different areas, and there is more to learn. On those days when I am tempted to strive harder to earn his love or approval, I realize I am asking the wrong question.

Instead of "Do I measure up?" the real question is "What measure of Jesus do I need today?"

When Mary first held her infant son, she was a young girl with very little experience in the ways of the world. She didn't know that one day she'd see him as a miracle worker. She experienced all the emotions that come with a close relationship: frustration, adoration, happiness, love. The relationship with her son, and later as her Savior, altered the direction of her life and transformed her as a woman.

Those revelations came with time and conversation and being in his presence.

The same is true for us.

When we first meet Jesus, we have no idea how that relationship will change us. That comes as we practice intimacy. We work through frustration. We learn to be truthful with him. We spend time with him. If we believe that we have to be perfect or be like someone else, we rule out authentic relationship.

When I first became a believer, I didn't come to faith because I wanted to be a more improved Suzie. I was not a DIY project, because "doing it yourself" was never his mission.

I ran to him because I experienced his love and it was irresistible. On the day that I first reached out to Jesus, he met me there and I wanted to know more. If you had asked me where my relationship with Christ would lead, I'd shrug my shoulders because I had no idea. I wasn't always sure of what to believe because I was so new in my faith. I didn't have much knowledge of theology or even the Bible. Realization came through relationship. I learned more about him layer by layer and year after year.

Layer by layer, year after year, I realized he knew me too.

This relationship produced restoration, for you can't be in proximity of Jesus and not be impacted by the Healer. I started to learn about his love as I received his love. I discovered that he was trustworthy, but only through trusting him.

I often felt challenged in my relationship with Jesus. At times I was frustrated by it. Sometimes my perception of him got a little twisted, and I tried to traipse down a rule-following route instead of a relationship. Jesus and I worked that out too.

As I learned about Jesus, I also learned about me.

JOY STEALER

Seeing your relationship with Christ as a DIY project.

There were things he already knew that I was just discovering. Like the fact that I took things personally. If I were to sit in a counselor's office, this trait would no doubt be traced back to my growing-up years. I believe in the power of godly counseling. As well, I know that as we sit in the presence of the Holy Spirit, he does a work. His fingerprints are on our spiritual DNA, and he sees the areas that need to be addressed as we grow. This isn't to punish us, but so we can step into who he knows we can be.

> You don't try to measure up, but reach for a greater measure of Jesus.

As JoyKeepers, we believe God knows who we are becoming. He's the one who created us, who knows the plans he has for us, and who will reveal who we are becoming. We don't expect perfection of ourselves, but we also don't resist uncomfortable paths that will help us mature in our faith.

As I saw that canyon-sized crack (of taking things personally), it became an invitation. I could wrestle with that for the rest of my days, or I could learn more about the way God made me, how my past shaped me, and how my faith plays out in all of that.

This was key to discovering who I really am, as well as whose I really am.

Start the Conversation

If you were to ask an acquaintance of mine to define me in one word, she might say *nice* or *kind* or *faith-filled*. Those words may fit, but if you were to ask my grandchildren the same question, their answers would be drastically different. To test that, I asked them this just the other day: *How would you describe Gaga in one word?*

Caleb (4): Goofy.

Jane (8): Silly.

Luke (8): Crazy.

Josiah (6): Definitely crazy.

Elle (9): I don't like to use the word crazy, so I choose fun.

Audrey (7): Very goofy.

These little humans know me better than almost anybody. Goofiness or silliness is a form of love language to me. There's no greater joke than that told by a six-year-old who can barely make it to the punchline. There's nothing more beautiful than falling to the floor, knees buckled as we laugh at a joke.

I named my little blue-green car Misty. She has "talked" to these littles since they were toddlers. We might be on our way to the store, when suddenly Misty tells them she wants ice cream. I try to talk her out of it, but she is insistent. As they get older, they realize who is in control of the car and the origin of the silly voice coming from the front seat, even as the littlest ones still believe that Misty is real. But they all love her and think she's in their corner. They fight to ride in Misty rather than in Richard's non-talking, non-ice-cream-loving vehicle.

Heaven help us if Misty is ever in a wreck and is totaled.

Do I do this with everyone? I don't. It's part of me, but with these little humans it's safe to let the goofy/crazy/silly side out because we have an authentic relationship.

I want you to do a quick exercise.

When we are asked to define ourselves, we usually try to downplay the good stuff or we miss those unique qualities that make us who we are. I chose my grandkids because they can't help but be honest.

- Take a few moments and ask this question of a handful of close friends or people who you trust and love you.
- Then make a list of the words they share.

This may feel vulnerable. That's okay. Feeling vulnerable is one of the most beautiful and hard markers of growth.

PAUSE POINT

Ask some people close to you to describe you in one or two words.

_____

_____

_____

Were you surprised by any of the words?

It's important that you don't discount the sweet or good words someone says over you.

I understand that there will be other words mixed in. I'm goofy or silly, but I also can get overtired and oversensitive. When we allow the positive words to blend with the work-in-progress areas, we get a more holistic view of who we are. If a hard word pops up and it stirs up an emotion, go back to the exercise in chapter 1 (page 27) and work through it.

God Speaks Words over You

I love this image of God portrayed by the prophet Zephaniah:

> For the Lord your God is living among you. He is a mighty savior. He will take delight in you with gladness. With his love, he will calm all your fears. He will rejoice over you with joyful songs.—Zephaniah 3:17 NLT

In this prophetic word, Zephaniah contrasts a rebellious people with a loving God. It's one of the most personal glimpses we have of God. It shows him as a Father. He is mighty, but he also takes joy in us. He offers rest from our fears. And the most beautiful part? God sings over us, his words flowing as we sleep, reminding us of who we are to him. When we tie our identity to an authentic relationship with him, an understanding develops.

He's not a distant God waiting to bring down thunder when we mess up.

He's close. He's attuned. He sees that we are tired of our striving ways and offers rest.

Are you ready for a second conversation?

This time it's between you and God.

It's a simple conversation. It's kind of fun, actually. You will share some things about yourself with him. Though he already knows these things about you, there's something holy that happens as you talk to him. Again, don't make this complicated.

Just let the words fall onto the page.

PAUSE POINT

Lord, I feel peaceful when . . .

_____

_____

_____

I feel closest to you (God) when . . .

_____

_____

_____

When I am in a crowd of new people, my reaction is . . .

_____

_____

_____

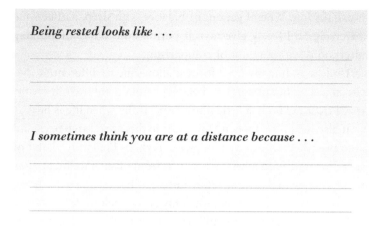

Being rested looks like . . .

I sometimes think you are at a distance because . . .

If I were doing this exercise just me and God, I'd share that I love nature. Sunrises and sunsets take my breath away. Water, especially the ocean or a gorgeous river, stirs something deep inside of me. Hiking and kayaking fill me up. Nature is my peaceful place.

I'd tell God that I feel closest to him when I worship him.

As far as people are concerned, I'm an introvert, so crowds are sweet for a short period of time, but I will need to fill back up. Over the years I have become more of an ambivert.

I am rested emotionally when my brain is a little less cluttered. Also, I need a certain number of hours of rest. I will never be the woman who only needs four hours of sleep. I will never be the woman who loves getting up at four a.m. It's not the way God wired me.

And the last question?

There are times I sense his presence powerfully, but there are seasons when I don't feel him. I'm pulled or overwhelmed or haven't spent time with him, so it feels unfamiliar. Even when I don't feel him, however, I'm reaching for him, because I know he's there.

As we share tidbits like this with God, it becomes an intimate moment. The Holy Spirit may even show you something you don't know. For example, I have learned that my Achilles' heel is exhaustion. When I get out of balance with sleep, it affects me adversely. So I freely give myself permission to nap on Sunday afternoons without guilt or comparison.

Understanding my need for rest allows me to differentiate between feeling out of sorts and being just plain old tired. It means that I treat my body a little more respectfully when life is busy.

It also means that when I fall short in this area, I step back and appraise where things went haywire. Perhaps I fell into a habit of spending time with a bright screen in front of my face night after night, then paid a price for it by not sleeping.

I can slip into condemnation at my cranky self or deal with the crux of the issue. No more phone at night for me. This girl needs sleep, and it's important for me to be kind to my people.

As we hold conversations like these with God, we hold up the traits he placed inside of us like a delighted child with a good, good Father.

Is this even spiritual? you might ask.

More than you can imagine.

Jesus met Peter and immediately changed his name to the Rock. He *knew* him. The longer that Peter walked with Jesus, the more he resembled Jesus's name for him.

When we believe that God knows who we are becoming, we exchange condemnation for connection. The more we learn about him, the greater we see his hand at work in us. This is not vanity, for he roots that out too. It's a spiritual revival where our heavenly Father heals old wounds, brings life to dead bones, and calls us to step into his plan for us.

We separate what we've been told and replace it with what is true. We shed words spoken over us that contradict what Jesus spoke. We leave behind tightly wound rules, which mimic religion, to obey him because we love and trust *him*.

This is a relationship of the best kind.

When we fall short, we know exactly where to go—not into judgment, but into mercy and a fresh start—because he knows us, he sees where that fall or fail originated, and together we get back up and start again.

Instead of trying to live for Jesus, we live *with* him.

That's a joy-changer!

Are you ready for one more conversation?

This one is much harder. Knowing how God made us is

JoyKeeper

Instead of striving to live for Jesus, you live with him.

beautiful, but there are things about us that didn't come from him. It's not the way he made us or intended for us. Instead, a response, feeling, or struggle was produced by the words or actions of others, or maybe even by our own decisions. Sharing this conversation digs a little deeper in the heart trenches.

Before you do this next exercise, will you pray this with me?

Father, you sent your Son with a mission to heal the broken-hearted and set the prisoner free. If there's even one chain wrapped around my heart or thoughts, you can break it. In fact, you already have. Help me to talk with you about those things that feel painful, or where I feel shame. Thank you that as I do, I am safe with you always. Thank you that as I do, you redeem and restore and will show me something new.

Don't allow an ounce of self-condemnation or guilt to enter this conversation. If that temptation arises, remind the enemy you are entering healing territory and he's not welcome.

PAUSE POINT

Lord, here are some hard things I want you to know about me:

_____

_____

_____

I was affected negatively by my past (an event or something someone said or did) and it shows up in me in this way:

_____

_____

_____

When I fall short, I respond by . . .

_____

_____

_____

This is one thing I want to do differently, with your help:

_____

_____

_____

#prayerstarter

Jesus, you know who I am becoming. Rather than run away from you, I'll run toward you because . . . [Finish this prayer in your own words.]

There's a good chance that after writing these things, you feel raw. One instinct may be to feel "bad" or exposed. That's not the voice of your Savior. Jesus said, "All those the Father gives me will come to me, and whoever comes to me I will never drive away" (John 6:37). *The Message* says, "I hold on and don't let go."

You bravely came to him in honesty. You went to the exact right place with these hurts and behaviors. He will never drive you away. He holds you tight. Not only that, but you may be unlocking a door to learn something new about yourself. The next time an adverse reaction or response rises up in you, there may be a deeper understanding of *why*.

This helps you know where to go and what to do differently.

These conversations with God also affect our human relationships. We learn to turn to God rather than ask a loved one to make that wound feel

> *JoyKeeper*
>
> When you believe that God knows who you are becoming, you exchange condemnation for connection.

better. If a friend messes up, we respond in relation to the actual offense instead of dragging in the cat of past hurts.

Knowing Jesus helps us know ourselves.

You are walking into the holy of holies without shame (Hebrews 4:16), with reverence, and in the power of relationship. Even in long-term relationships there are times when we realize our need for increased intimacy. That's what you are doing right now. He already knows every ounce of what you are showing him, and there's power in the sharing.

Real Life

Pretend you have a remote in your hand. Let's rewind. A toddler pokes me in the eye with a fork. I get him a spoon, and he throws it on the floor. We sit at the table and he's mad because he wants the fork. A friend walks by and says, "What are you doing to that baby?" I offer a half smile. After all, she is only teasing. She says something else, and then there's another little poke.

"I'm not doing anything to him," I say. My tone is defensive.

On the surface this seems like an obvious scene. Surely what is taking place is that my friend is insensitive. I almost received a fork to the eye!

That's not her intention, however. She's being playful.

There are all kinds of responses that could take place. I could offer a snarky response, which is where I felt myself heading. I could lash out. I could feel like a failure. I could isolate. I could decide I'm never going to see that person again. I could talk to someone else about how awful a friend she is. I could take it out on the toddler (I wouldn't, but it's an option).

At the core of this, her teasing hit a tender nerve.

It's that nerve that says, "You don't measure up."

There's a good chance you didn't almost get a fork in the eye today. Perhaps you are exhausted in ministry and that one woman is making you feel a little crazy. Maybe you have this dream to do something, and it's not happening like you think it should. You look around and see others succeeding, and it makes you wonder if you've missed a step.

I don't know what measuring stick you are holding up today, but if it is making you feel like you are not enough, would you consider a different response?

Instead of leading with your hurt, what if you led with your healing?

Okay, Lord, I'm feeling all kinds of feelings right now. Help me to know myself in this moment, because no one knows me better than you.

This is the practice of intimacy. It breaks all kinds of unhealthy unspoken rules like, "Once you start to mess up, you're already too far gone," or, "If you aren't going to measure up, why try?"

This practice of intimacy crushes condemnation. I was overstimulated. My friend was just being playful. The toddler was little and tired. None of this had anything to do with measuring up. It was a need to deal with what was taking place in that moment.

In my heart. In my body. In my soul.

JOY STEALER

Focusing on where you are not rather than on how far you've come.

My response was actually *not* to respond but to take the little one to a parent, who knew exactly what to do. It was also to slip away for a few moments and take a deep breath.

If this feels foreign or even hard to you, sprinkle grace into the process. Knowing ourselves takes time and practice. Intimacy with God takes time and takes inviting him into both the good and the hard moments. We learn as we fall on our face and get back up—and going to Jesus and talking about that. We grow as we forgive ourselves and others.

JoyKeeper

Knowing Jesus helps you know yourself.

We march into our real identity as we stop trying to measure up to anyone's expectations other than God's.

JoyKeeper:
Offer Yourself Grace As You Transform

Truth

He decided from the outset to shape the lives of those who love him along the same lines as the life of his Son. The Son stands first in the line of humanity he restored. We see the original and intended shape of our lives there in him. After God made that decision of what his children should be like, he followed it up by calling people by name. After he called them by name, he set them on a solid basis with himself. And then, after getting them established, he stayed with them to the end, gloriously completing what he had begun.

So, what do you think? With God on our side like this, how can we lose?—Romans 8:29–31 MESSAGE

Live It

- Bring your shortcomings to him rather than hide because of them.
- When you feel wounded, ask God to show you why.
- Before reacting, pause for five seconds to ask the Lord to help you respond as a healed woman.

When we stop trying to measure up, it breaks manmade barricades between ourselves and God. We open the door to life-changing conversation rather than beat ourselves up. Our words are kinder not only to ourselves but to others. Today, write a note or send a text to a friend, a child, or a family member and let them know that you delight in a trait that is unique to them.

Jesus, I am a healed woman! I know there's more healing ahead, and I am excited about that too. Continue to do a good work in me. Show me what I do not see. Let me bring my wounds to the light, not out of condemnation but because there's good you want to do in me. Amen.

three

chalk-line faith

magine a woman who juggles constantly. She never puts the balls down, though sometimes they fall on their own.

She is on guard 24/7 making sure those she loves never hurt, fail, or fall.

She worries about the condition of the world, but she isn't sure what to do, which means there are days she think will implode—or explode.

She's a great mom. A good friend. She tends to carry a disproportionate load in relationships or tasks. She is known as sacrificial. People aren't afraid to ask her for help because there is a good chance she'll say yes—even when no is screaming in her brain.

People-pleasing, pressure, and persistence are her kryptonite.

Asking for help? *That's not her way.*

Admitting that all her efforts don't always work out the way she wants? *Well, okay.*

Attempting to carry the weight of the world? *Doesn't everybody?*

Blaming herself when things go wrong, even if it isn't her fault? *Check.*

This strong, amazing woman is tired with a capital T. Sleep is elusive because that's when she makes her longest lists or goes over her day wishing it had gone better or smoother.

Life often feels chaotic because it *is* chaotic.

Maybe it will be better tomorrow.

Truth #3: God is God, and you are not.

WHAT I FEEL: **It's my job to fix everything.**
WHAT I KNOW: **God is God, and I am not.**

The God who made the world and everything in it is the Lord of heaven and earth and does not live in temples built by human hands. And he is not served by human hands, as if he needed anything. Rather, he himself gives everyone life and breath and everything else.—Acts 17:24–25

I texted with several friends recently and asked two questions:

1. Do you ever feel overwhelmed?
2. What does that look like?

It didn't take but a few seconds for my phone to start popping with their answers. These were a few of their responses:

I feel overwhelmed by an overloaded schedule.
I feel overwhelmed by a marriage going the wrong direction.
I feel overwhelmed by my teenager who is making poor decisions.
I feel overwhelmed by my thoughts that are supercritical.
I am overwhelmed as I struggle with chronic illness.
I am overwhelmed as I get older.

I'm overwhelmed by all the negative news. I just want it to stop already.

I was stunned by the honesty of their responses. It felt like a divine conversation. As women spoke their truth, friends started to ping back with affirmation.

Me too, sis.

Wow, I thought I was the only one.

The conversation continued through the next day. The list grew as women shared how they felt overwhelmed as they loved aging parents, dealt with energetic children, waded through the angst of social media, experienced deep caverns of loss, fought to put their phones down, felt in limbo, struggled financially, prepared to move, anticipated transition, managed busyness, and so much more.

JoyKeeper

When you affirm your struggle with a good friend, neither of you feels alone.

Whew.

Asking two simple questions broke open a well.

As we talked, it became clear that all of us feel overwhelmed at one time or another. Life *will* be chaotic. The problem arises when we can't fix or control those messy happenings. The joy stealer woven all throughout the conversation wasn't merely about a situation, a person, or an ongoing event, but about the chaos it produced *in* each of us.

Jesus experienced chaos too. In Matthew 11, a long, difficult day is underway. John the Baptist is in prison and chock-full of hard questions for Jesus. Additionally, Jesus's words have fallen on fallow ground all day long. Blind eyes are opened. The lame walk. The deaf hear, but still people resist his message.

Jesus stands in front of the multitude. He describes how fickle people can be (vv. 16–20). One minute singing his praises, the next complaining and nitpicking. They are hungry for signs and miracles, but not for repentance. They want religion over relationship with God. Suddenly, in the middle of his message, Jesus does something unexpected.

He halts the conversation to talk to his heavenly Father (vv. 25–27).

Now, I want you to imagine this. You are at a conference and the main speaker is engaged in the message. The spotlight is shining. Everyone is tuned in.

Then, without warning, the speaker stops speaking and starts talking to God.

Maybe, like the crowd watching Jesus, you wonder what in the world is going on.

There are days I hit the end of me, and God is the only place I know to go. I wonder if Jesus felt the same way. As he prays, he reveals that it's indeed been a hard day, but God is sovereign. The wise and learned may reject his message, but his heavenly Father will unfold his plan through the unlearned, the unlikely, and in unexpected ways.

God is God, and his plans are greater.

Was that message for the crowd? *Perhaps.* But it was also for Jesus.

Hebrews 2:18 (NLT) reminds us that "since he himself has gone through suffering and testing, he is able to help us when we are being tested." Jesus faced discouragement. Sometimes people, even those closest to him, let him down. If Jesus hit a brick wall, then we will sometimes hit one too. If Jesus found himself depleted or hovering on empty, we will too.

If Jesus had to stop in the middle of what he was doing to connect to a greater Source, maybe that's something we need as well.

Letting Go of Our List

I can't tell you how many times I've been on task.

Jesus, I'm asking for help in this area, but just in case, here's my plan . . .

   . . . to offer wisdom,

   . . . to show up as an accountability partner,

   . . . to support through the hard days ahead,

   . . . to manage what might go wrong.

The tricky thing about my list is that it looks like caring, except it's based on control. Actually, it's based on fear of being out of control. I'm asking for God's help, but I'd really like it to be in my timing. I want to see progress.

I don't want to have to trust, especially if it's not going the way I want.

Joy Keeper

Rather than ask God to change a circumstance, you ask him to meet you in the midst of it.

Imagine the balls flying through the air. Fast. Hard. Swirling around me.

Of course, there's a good chance I'll drop one . . . and then another. They might all come tumbling down, because honestly, there isn't much I can control about someone else's circumstances or choices. If a ball falls, I scramble to pick it up and maybe add another two or three in there while I'm at it.

Because this is what we are tempted to do.

It was hard to admit that my "helping" didn't always accomplish what I hoped. In fact, most of the time it left me feeling defeated. A long time ago I sensed God asking me to put the balls down and stop making lists. It's not that I didn't have an assignment, but it was never to hold the world together.

Instead of juggling all the balls, what if we choose to stop like Jesus did?

God, show me what to do. Show me what not to do.

Though I have a plan, I surrender to your plan, for it is greater and higher than mine.

As we do this, the wisdom tumbling into our hearts might not be what we expect. There may be specific things we are to do, but we might hear these words instead:

This is not your assignment.

Over the years I've come to call this chalk-line faith.

Picture a chalk line drawn around your feet. Everything within that chalk line is something you *can* do. You can pray. You can be present. You can love. Everything outside of that chalk line is either God's assignment or falls squarely in someone else's territory. I can't begin to tell you how many times chalk-line faith has rescued me from myself.

Words rest on the tip of my tongue ready to be released into the wild. I've already prayed about it and sense this particular task isn't mine. I'm poised to do it anyway, because doing something feels right.

Then I imagine that chalk line being gently redrawn around my feet.

I take those non-Suzie assignments—with a friend, a loved one, a neighbor—to my Savior and put them down . . . again.

Helpful or Not?

When we put down assignments that aren't ours, we are released to do the assignments that are. Healthy things. Helpful things (not defined by a need to fix). In the year called scarred, I didn't know what the future held. I wasn't sure if everything was going to be okay.

All I had was the Holy Spirit.

Then one day it's like I woke up from a stupor.

Oh my word, all I have is the Holy Spirit!

Jesus often comforted his friends by reminding them of the Holy Spirit's power in their life. He told them the Holy Spirit would tell them what to say (Luke 12:12). They discovered the Holy Spirit would direct them and offer discernment. They couldn't control every situation. They couldn't manage people according to their specifications. They didn't always know what to do, but the Holy Spirit was in them and would lead them.

> **JOY STEALER**
> Being on guard 24/7 to make sure those you love never hurt, fail, or fall.

He empowered them in the midst of that messy situation.

As we release those things that aren't our assignments, we receive direction. It might be to pray. It might be to encourage. Sometimes it's setting healthy boundaries while loving that person.

> **JoyKeeper**
>
> When you put down assignments that aren't yours, you are released to do an assignment that is yours.

Whatever it might be, it's not born out of a need to control or manage, but comes from releasing that situation or person (as well as our own hearts) into the hands of God. We are available and ready to do our assignment, but not out of fear—rather, out of faith.

Chalk-Line Faith Is Freedom

When we are trying to be all and do all, we set ourselves up for failure. We take on God-sized tasks that knock us down. We play the blame game when it doesn't work, and the finger is usually pointed square at our own heart.

As you walk in chalk-line faith, God is doing a work in others, but don't underestimate the work he is doing in you. On those days when everything within you is trying to hold up the world, you are free to do what God is asking and no more. You are free to love to the best of your ability. You are free to offer truth, when it is your assignment to do so, but it's not your job to make anyone receive it.

You show up, but you don't have to hold up the whole stinking world.

You are free to bring the weight of the burden to the Lord and find the rest so badly needed. You are also freed to get out of God's way so he can do his job.

If you believe that without your intervention everything will fall apart, you've placed expectations on yourself that are greater than what God is asking.

Just as Jesus stopped in the midst of chaos and looked to his heavenly Father, do the same. Remind yourself of his promises. Thank him for the ongoing work, even when it's unseen.

I asked that same group of friends—the ones who shared what made them feel overwhelmed—another question: What is one assignment God is giving you today?

A friend texted back, "Okay, Suz. This is hard. I've been so focused on the chaos and how it's making me feel that I never thought to ask this question." So she did. She got alone with God in prayer and held up the entire situation to him. She asked if he would cut through the clutter of her feelings and speak to her.

The simple answer came.

Be honest.

In her case, her assignment was to be honest with family members who had created chaos for a long time. It was also to be honest with herself about how she had been contributing to the chaos, though meaning well. Last, she needed to honest about the fact that what she had been doing wasn't working.

Focusing on that one assignment felt like a cool rain after a scorching summer. She tackled her new assignment. It started with an honest conversation with her family. It wasn't easy, but it released resentment that had built for months.

Her words didn't have to be received right away. It might take time. After all, this was a brand-new waltz between them. There was an established pattern, and breaking it was uncomfortable for all involved. There was a chance they might not appreciate her words at all. Her responsibility was simply to speak those words in love and after prayer.

> **JOY STEALER**
>
> The thought that without your intervention, everything will fall apart.

Her next assignment was to take a look at all the things piled up on her to-do plate in regard to this situation. It was time for some of those to come off.

- If it wasn't healthy, it didn't get to stay.
- If it enabled, it came off.
- If it caused friction in her own family, it needed a second look. It would either be removed or be changed.

Last, she was invited to examine her own frustration at the situation. It's not uncommon to point at another person or complex circumstance as the source of our frustration and completely ignore what we bring to the mix.

What If It's a Good Thing?

Recently I stepped away from a beautiful ministry in which I served for fourteen years. A few months earlier, I had felt the passion ebbing. It was like wearing a heart monitor and, one by one, the plugs were being pulled. When I prayed about it, I sensed it was time. It was hard to put this down because it was such a "good" thing. I loved the people involved. This ministry had a huge reach and allowed me to come alongside women all over the world.

Putting down something good can feel harder.

It would be a lot easier to shut this door if I was mad at someone. The day after I stepped away, however, I took a deep breath. While my calendar was still full, I saw margin ahead. Over the next few weeks, new opportunities filtered in through my inbox. It's my instinct to fill up my calendar, especially with good things. This means I needed to assess each opportunity as it came. It might look good, but was it my assignment? I said no to a couple sweet opportunities right away. I said yes to a couple of new assignments that had nothing to do with work or ministry but focused on family.

The small shift in margin was a time of refueling and redirection.

If I had held on to the original "good" thing, I would have missed what God was trying to give me.

If I had filled up the margins with other opportunities right away (without prayerfully looking at each one), I would have found myself back where I began, swimming in an ocean of assignments, some mine, some not.

Let's stop for a moment and answer the question I asked my friends.

These are the questions I ask myself when I feel those balls flying through the air and realize I've done it again.

PAUSE POINT

Do I feel overwhelmed, and what does that feel like?

_____

_____

_____

What are all the balls that I'm juggling?

_____

_____

_____

Is there a ball I'm juggling that's not mine? Am I taking on someone else's assignment? (It might be God's. It might be another person's. This is not an invitation to define whose assignment it is, just to clarify that it's not yours.)

_____

_____

_____

Now let's ask another important question.

Lord, what is my one *assignment in the midst of this situation, in this season, or with this person?*

_____

_____

_____

The answer may come like a rush and surprise you with its simplicity. It may unfold over the next few days or weeks.

Keep asking.

Whatever the answer is, remember this: God is God, and you are not—and that's a really good thing.

He Knows Where He's Taking You

A few years ago, cynicism crept into my heart like a virus. The world felt incredibly messed up. I recognized the Holy Spirit tugging at me with a now familiar question.

What is your assignment?

It wasn't to fix the world, because, well, that's impossible. It also wasn't to keep obsessing over all the things I couldn't do. When I asked God to show me my one thing, it was this:

Find the good that people are doing and encourage them.

I intentionally began to read about people doing good in the world. Some led Bible studies in prison. Others rocked babies as mamas went through rehabilitation. Some hosted literacy programs, food banks, or compassionate employment. Literally, there was good all around me, and I had almost missed it.

I kept my assignment in front of me. I wasn't sure what that looked like, but I was open.

Eventually I felt God leading me to create a series of projects to bring awareness and funding to some of these ministries. This became a part of my ministry called Toget*her*.[1]

With the help of other women around the nation, we funded literacy classes for women in India who had never learned to read. We raised funds for equipment for a ministry that offers community and dignity to once-exploited women. We wrapped arms around refugee families with much-needed dental care. We came alongside an organization that offers community for pregnant women who are homeless or almost homeless.

I had no idea this was even a possibility, but God did.

You never know where your assignment may lead you.

God led me into my assignment but led me out of cynicism.

My one assignment wasn't to wring my hands over the messiness of the world. It wasn't to stew about all the things that were wrong.

I might still be there, juggling all the balls that weren't mine to juggle, when he had an assignment of freedom for me.

Stepping into your assignment may lead to rest, which leads to laughter, which leads to stronger and healthier relationships. Stepping into your assignment may lead to white space on your calendar, and you step into that gifting you've never had time to develop. Stepping into your assignment may lead you to trust, and that's one of the most faith-impacting paths we take.

JOY STEALER

Placing expectations on yourself that are greater than what God is asking.

---

1. Learn more about Toget*her* at tsuzanneeller.com/together-projects.

Real Life

Trying to take care of the whole world is exhausting. As you place down those assignments that are not yours, may I suggest an assignment that is?

Take care of you.

This may not feel spiritual or biblical to you, but we often see Jesus pulling away from the crowd to rest or pray. His days were long. His mission was huge. But he showed us the power of filling back up.

When I talk with women about taking care of themselves, I often hear responses like these:

That feels selfish.

Who has time for that?

My job is to take care of my family.

I don't even know what that looks like.

Let's tackle those one by one.

This feels selfish.

To be selfish is to be self-centered and self-seeking. That's not what we are talking about. Rather, we nurture ourselves, so we can pour back out. Jesus often sought a solitary place to pray after a long day of ministry. He also surrounded himself with friends.

What fills you up? Is it reading a chapter of a good book? Is it worship? Is it nature or music or a really delicious taco? Maybe it's laughter with a good friend or getting away for a couple of hours with a loved one.

Do that thing.

Who has time for that?

We make time for things all the time. We squeeze in one more appointment. We take on one more task.

Of course, there are times when it's much more difficult.

Ask for help when it's needed. It might be one hour a week or every other week.

A nap, a walk, or coffee with a good friend might feel like an extravagance, but if it fills you back up it's a win in your relationships, and in your current assignments.

My job is to take care of . . .

I get it. I have that same list.

A few of my jobs are to take care of paying the bills. Clean the house. Meet book and ministry deadlines. Show up for aging parents. Love my grandbabies. Give my own children a break occasionally as they parent. From time to time, the list changes as I take on tasks when Richard is in a busy season. Other times he shifts to take some of mine.

I didn't list all my tasks. If I did, it could feel overwhelming.

But adding one more assignment is important.

My assignment is to take care of me.

If we wait to nurture our body and soul, chances are we'll be withered up and dog-tired. Chances are we'll be cranky, even as we try not to be. Discovering what we love, what fills us up, and how to do that on a regular basis is life-changing. One good book, one short walk, one dance around the living room, or one garden-planting session at a time.

I don't even know what that looks like.

While reading and having a solitary afternoon fill me up, being with people is what fills up my husband. He learned that he doesn't have to have a structured invitation to be with friends. If we waited for that in this busy season, it might never happen. When he needs a people fill-up, he texts a couple friends of ours to ask if they want to take a walk around a nearby trail. Sometimes they can. Sometimes they are unable. When it works, it's fun.

JoyKeeper

When you allow God to lead you out of an assignment that isn't yours, he leads you into joy.

What do you love to do that is low-key and doable? You don't have to have a plan, unless planning makes you happy. Then plan away. The important thing is to nurture yourself so you can carry out those assignments that feel so big.

JoyKeeper:
Release What Is Not Your Assignment

Truth

I became a servant of this gospel by the gift of God's grace given me through the working of his power.—Ephesians 3:7

Live It

- Clearly define the balls you aren't supposed to juggle.
- When tempted to take God's place in another person's life, draw an imaginary chalk line.

New behaviors take time to develop. You will pick up those non-assigned balls and start juggling again. You will step out of that chalk line. When that happens, be really nice to yourself, then . . .

Reassess.

Reassign.

Rest.

Then start fresh.

Jesus, you understand what it feels like to be exhausted—by people, by long days, by the "bigness" of all that needs to be accomplished. You also know the heart of God. Over me. Over my loved ones. You have an assignment just for me in this season. I say yes to it and nothing else. In Jesus's name, amen.

part two

Keeping Joy

You are a JoyKeeper in the making.
You are a keeper of truth.
You don't measure joy by temporary circumstances and feelings.
You grasp who (and whose) you are.
You are trusting God.

Now, let's continue to discover what you never knew about joy.
You have a safe place, always.
You will shun shame.
There's a place for you. Oh yes, there is.

four

a safe place

It was supposed to be a fun evening with friends. Some counseling peers of Richard's were hosting a marriage seminar. They invited a handful of people to participate in a two-day mock marriage retreat.

Our role was to offer feedback on the new program.

Included in this invitation was dinner at a local Mexican restaurant and fun with good people.

Win-win, right?

The first night we participated in the seminar, just as other couples would in coming weeks. The teaching was insightful and challenging.

This is going to be great for couples, I thought.

Other couples. Other people.

Then a video titled "Still Face" started playing on the screen. Maybe you've seen it. In the video a baby interacts with her mother. She sits in a high chair and her mama sits in front of her. They laugh. They touch. The little girl reaches for her mama's face and her mama reaches back. It's beautiful.

Until it's not.

The mother's face goes still. Not angry. Not harsh. Just still. She stares at her daughter. There is no more touching. No more connection.

The little girl reaches for her mama. There is no response. She tries harder. Her mother simply gazes at her. The child arches her back, squeals loudly, and twists in her seat. Her hands flail. She's in distress. Finally, the mother breaks her "still face." She eagerly reaches for her child. Her words are soothing. The little one relaxes. Her world is right again.

Mine was not.

I was shattered. Tears drenched my face. I clutched a ragged tissue. Richard sat quietly beside me. It's not that he was unmoved, but it didn't affect him the same way.

"Suzie, can you share what you are feeling right now?" our friend, the host, asked.

No. Not just no, but unequivocally no.

I didn't trust myself to speak, so I simply shook my head.

When the session ended, Richard and I climbed into the car. We sat in the darkness for a few moments. He had witnessed the tears but wasn't sure what was going on.

I didn't understand it myself, but I tried to explain.

The relationship between daughter and mother was beautiful. The little girl felt loved and the bond was strong. While others may have felt a sense of relief when the mother reached for her, it made me angry.

You just don't do that. You can't be a safe place and then rip it away.

This video marched into old places where I once ached.

Truth #4: God is your safe place.

WHAT I FEEL: Insecure (unsafe).
WHAT I KNOW: God is my safe place.

God is a safe place to hide, ready to help when we need him. We stand fearless at the cliff-edge of doom, courageous in seastorm and earthquake, before the rush and roar of oceans, the tremors that shift mountains.—Psalm 46:1–2 MESSAGE

Once we become believers, we should always feel safe. Protected. Strong. We should never struggle with insecurity.

Right?

No, friend. For if this were true, I would have been disqualified long ago. I *am* a strong woman, and there's a good chance you'd describe yourself the same way.

This particular joy stealer is subtle. We can be tooling along, doing just fine, when out of the blue we feel unsafe, out in the open, unprotected, defenseless, and insecure. It might be tied to a person or an incident. It might pop up out of nowhere, and we wonder what in the world is going on.

That's how I felt that day in the marriage seminar. That video triggered something deep inside of me, bringing me all the way back to my childhood. The tears were real and so were the feelings.

I could run from them or run toward them. That moment became an opportunity to examine why I felt the way I did and hopefully to understand where the feelings came from. This led to a deeper layer of healing and understanding in an area I didn't even know still needed God's touch.

More than any other in this book, I wrestled with this chapter. It was written and rewritten and written again. It's demoralizing when a woman struggles with insecurity in any form, and someone says, "You shouldn't feel that way." It's harder still when Scripture is tacked onto that statement, because suddenly you not only feel insecure, but that you are falling short as a believer.

Can I tell you something? You *are* strong. You love the Lord with all of your heart and he knows that better than anyone.

We all need a safe place. Sometimes we simply walk out our faith every day and that is beautiful, but sometimes we run to God in a storm. That's wisdom because a storm shelter is the smartest place to be when lightning is crackling across the sky and it feels dark or uncertain.

So what might that safe place look like?

In the last chapter, I shared a story from Matthew 11.

Let's continue that story.

If you remember, Jesus has experienced a really hard day. He's speaking to a multitude when, out of the blue, he starts talking to his heavenly Father. There is a clear note of joy as Jesus shifts from disheartened to what he *knows* to be true, which is that God is sovereign. A series of faith statements spoken by Jesus does something in his heart.

Then he issues an invitation to the crowd.

> Come to me, all who labor and are heavy laden, and I will give you rest. Take my yoke upon you, and learn from me, for I am gentle and lowly in heart, and you will find rest for your souls. For my yoke is easy, and my burden is light.—Matthew 11:28–30 ESV

Jesus understands exactly what it feels like to be doing everything "right" and to still feel unsettled or uncertain, but he also knows the extraordinary depths of rest to be found in our heavenly Father.

He looks out over the crowd, just as he looks into our eyes, and offers supernatural rest. I can only imagine the deep breath this allowed many in that crowd. It's the same exhale I have experienced when I have reached that storm shelter and settled in to find what I need.

This rest is the opposite of a do-more, try-harder, you-should-never-feel-this-way mentality. Rather than ask us to do more, he requests we come to him directly. Don't pass go. Don't stop along the way.

This invitation is twofold. It's for those who labor and for those who are heavy-laden.

When we feel uncertain or unsafe in our faith, we might turn to labor. We shoulder the blame. We pick up stones of rejection. We create an impossible standard in our faith. While we offer grace to everyone else, we have little for ourselves.

A person who is heavy-laden is someone who is carrying a burden someone else put on them.

Both are exhausting.

All we know is we are tired from the inside out.

His rest is our safe place.

The word *rest* in this invitation is translated from the Greek *anapausis*. This is spiritual rest that goes deep into the heart, thought life, and well-being of the one who receives it. It's rest that gives intermission from the laborious work of worry, condemnation, and rigorous religious standards.

It's rest from old wounds and unhealthy or manmade teaching.

This isn't rest *from* something, but rest *in* something.

This rest syncs us with the being and heart of God.

When we receive this rest, we begin to find refuge (a safe place).

When we find refuge, we find stability in love that isn't hinged on our mistakes or the mistakes of others.

We are still human. We are still works in progress, but we know where to turn. We aren't afraid to look deep to find roots of insecurity that may be lingering.

This safe place of rest is not shaky. It doesn't depend on performance. It's not a test. It's not based on a person's perception of you, or what someone thinks you should or shouldn't do. It doesn't judge you.

Instead, we rest in the truth that we are loved. There is no other version of this story. That is our safe place.

An Honest Look

Deep insecurity often has deep roots. One of the sweetest places to explore those roots is in the presence of a God who loves us more than we can imagine. This has the power to move us from insecurity to understanding.

Let's look at four things that can contribute to feeling unsafe.

1. Misunderstanding God's Character

I wish this wasn't an issue, but sometimes we feel insecure in our faith. We believe we fall short of God's love or affection. We believe trying harder is what God demands. This creates the illusion of a tenuous relationship. It makes one of the best gifts—our faith— feel less than safe.

We start off walking with him daily. We feel his presence. We know how good this relationship can be, because we have experienced it.

And then we fall short in some way. It might be big. It might be small. It might not even be a mistake, but the belief that we've missed the bar. That sets off a reaction similar to the "still face" interaction between the little girl and her mother.

God is not like the mother in the video. It's not who he is or what his Word says, but it's what we believe is taking place.

We were in sync; everything was great. And now it's not.

> **JOY STEALER**
> The belief that trying harder, striving more, is what God demands.

That sets us into motion. We try harder. We pray extra. We tap dance as fast as we can to get his attention.

See me, God?

I'm here. Dancing away. Working as hard as I know how.

I'm the worst Christian/mom/wife/friend/person ever.

I'll do better next time.

Do you see me yet?

We feel not only uncertain, but spiritually exhausted.

As I wrote this chapter, the Holy Spirit drew me back to this one fact over and over again.

> **JoyKeeper**
> You understand that God loves you, and there is no other version of this story.

There are too many faith-filled, much-loved daughters of God who live as if God loves them, loves them not.

They are trapped in a work harder, try-more cycle. This cycle leads to living defeated, because if one mistake can spiral you out of God's affection or approval, faith feels impossible.

This belief system is exhausting, and it's not his best for us.

2. A Bullying Inner Critic

A couple of years ago, a group of friends and I studied the Enneagram system, which sorts people into nine distinct personality types. It's fascinating to see how God so uniquely created each of us. A few of my friends are type one, the Perfectionist or Reformer. They are described as conscientious and ethical. They care a lot about excellence, so they are great to have on your team.

They also have a tough inner critic. While self-disciplined, wise, and fair, they may fear making a mistake. They constantly consider ways to make something better, but they might also rehearse what went wrong over and over again.

Tests like these reveal that some of us are naturally wired with an inner critic. It's part of the unique way that God created us.

Understanding the strengths of this is key. If you naturally have a strong inner critic, there's a good chance you also have a strong sense of justice. You reach for excellence. You examine things a little more deeply than others, and your insight can be a gift.

But the problem arises when that inner critic turns into a bully.

I spent a week at the home of a close friend. Our goal was to brainstorm our next book projects, and also to have fun.

Late one night, a smoke alarm beeped. The alarm was wired into a whole-house system, and there were numerous alarms on both stories of the house. Before long the beeps turned into a full-blown siren. Like, a blast-your-ears-off siren that went off every ten minutes or so. Downstairs, the device cried, "Fire, fire, fire!"

It was so ridiculous it was almost funny.

There was no fire or smell of smoke. We were in a remote area. There wasn't anything we could do, so we climbed into our respective beds, put in earplugs, covered our heads with pillows, and tried to sleep.

At one thirty in the morning, a knock came at my bedroom door. My friend had called the fire department, and they were on the way. The thought occurred to her that it may not be a fire, but it could be something like a carbon monoxide leak.

That's when I noticed her tears.

She had been awake the whole time, and her inner critic was in full-blown bully mode.

She told me how sorry she was that things had gone wrong.

All I could think of was how amazing she had been. She had hosted, fed, and created a welcoming environment. One uncomfortable night didn't discount all the sweet laughter and fun we'd had. A firefighter arrived, and within a few minutes the offending alarm was silenced.

When we gathered the next day on the back deck, overlooking the gorgeous mountain view, my friend talked about the night before. She shared that her inner critic told her she had fallen short. It was all hinged on expectations. Though the week had been so great, somehow all of that was eclipsed by one thing going awry.

An inner critic, when it's in the bully stage, is loud and clanging. It draws a fine line between approved and not. Every mistake (even if it isn't our responsibility) holds the possibility of guilt.

It would be easy for any of us to just say, "Don't do that."

What a travesty that would be.

For most women who battle an inner critic, this is their greatest wish. They fight that critic daily. They are on the front lines in this battle. To say, "Just don't do it," adds to the burden already carried by those whose inner critic is loud, persistent, and wearying.

As my friend and I talked, it was enlightening. She understood that the burden was hinged on unrealistic expectations. She understood the strengths of this inner voice, but also that it crossed the line from a strength to a bully at times. Though it had knocked her around the night before, it didn't get the last word.

Truth did.

By talking about it, she was able to hear those unrealistic expectations out loud. We were able to bring other aspects of the weekend into the picture—lots of laughter, pints of ice cream, long hikes and a waterfall, and lots of clarity on future writing projects.

If you have an inner critic that is a bully, don't ignore it but don't try to battle alone. Join it with a Scripture. Take it to that place of rest and put it down. Share it with a friend and listen to what she has to say.

Let's do that together right now.

PAUSE POINT

The inner critic is saying . . .

_____

_____

_____

What does God's Word say about this?

_____

_____

What does a close friend or loved one say about it?

_____

_____

_____

Does this change the narrative? If so, how?

_____

_____

_____

3. Bad Theology

While there are thousands of life-giving churches and people around the world, there are also those who try to control others through tangled and twisted beliefs. I've been in ministry for twenty years and have wept over "truth" that kept people in bondage rather than set them free.

Bad theology weaponizes Scripture to keep a believer in line.

Bad theology isn't about Jesus. It's about people.

This is the type of doctrine the Pharisees carried out in the New Testament, and Jesus laid it wide open over and again. While their motivation was to live a holy life, the path to faith they offered was rife with complicated laws, rules, and regulations. The people under this bad theology not only fell in their religion but fell short with those in authority. Jesus climbed on a cross for us because this system didn't work.

This type of faith rates sin, and it's confusing. It tells you God can't use you, not until you hit a certain standard—*theirs*.

The truth is that none of us are "good" in our own being.

When Jesus offered rest for those who were heavy-laden, he was describing people weighed down by the burden of bad theology—a burden placed on us by someone else. It's a measuring stick so out of reach that we may never stop trying to attain it.

The stunning message Jesus taught through his life, death, and resurrection was that he is the way to the Father (John 14:6). There is no other way.

Jesus invites ordinary people with all kinds of flaws to join him. Our relationship with him changes us. Jesus is our ultimate refuge.

Can we just admit that bad theology exists? When someone tells you that God "loves you, loves you not," it flies in the face of Scriptures like this:

> What shall we say about such wonderful things as these? If God is for us, who can ever be against us? Since he did not spare even his own Son but gave him up for us all, won't he also give us everything else? Who dares accuse us whom God has chosen for his own? No one—for God himself has given us right standing with himself. Who then will condemn us? No one—for Christ Jesus died for us and was raised to life for us, and he is sitting in the place of honor at God's right hand, pleading for us.—Romans 8:31–34 NLT

If any doctrine leads to doubt, dig deeper.

If theology flies in the face of a Savior who came to mend the broken hearted, set the prisoner free, and liberate those in strongholds, and also had good news for those impoverished in body or spirit, there are other churches and small groups that will welcome you.

If you fear your questions will make someone mad or place you outside a certain circle, that's a flashing red light. There will never be a perfect church, for every church is filled with messy humans like you and me, but there is a distinction between an abusive doctrine and the message Jesus taught (and lived).

Sometimes we turn away from Jesus because of his people.

Never, ever allow a work-in-progress human to keep you from the One who loves you most. This isn't judging. It is simply removing that person's voice from the mix.

His voice is the one you listen to and the one that guides your faith.

4. Upbringing

Amy Carroll is a close friend and the co-author of *Exhale*. In her book, she tells a story of her friend Amber, who had to deal with unhealthy interactions with a close relative. These interactions left her wounded every time.

As I read Amy's book, I took a deep breath when Amber likened these interactions to a "plate of trash."

> "Sometimes my relative hands me a plate of trash," Amber told me. "My whole life, I've accepted the plate she's handed to me as if I now actually own it, saying, 'Of course I'll take your trash. *Thank you* for this plate of trash!'"[1]

Some of us grew up receiving a plate of trash. Unkind and unjust words. Unfair comparisons. This is when we can feel heavy-laden, just as Jesus described. We aren't carrying our own junk, but the rubbish of someone else's brokenness.

Recognizing those words and actions in that way changed things for Amber. When this person offered disparaging words, that trash wasn't Amber's to keep.

It was the other person's trash to hold or throw away.

1. Amy Carroll and Cheri Gregory, *Exhale: Lose Who You're Not, Love Who You Are, Live Your One Life Well* (Minneapolis: Bethany House, 2019), 42.

There's a lot of wisdom in this analogy. A lot of us are holding on to garbage we were given long ago. Maybe through a parent, a sibling, or a spouse. It can come from friends or co-workers. This garbage might be as recent as yesterday, but often it's stinking and moldy because it was handed to us decades ago.

Yet we hold on.

What if we lovingly hand back that trash?

What if we take those words spoken over us long ago—that we will never measure up, we aren't thin enough, we aren't smart enough, we aren't like our sibling, we will never make anything of ourselves—and see them as rubbage?

JoyKeeper

If doctrine led you to doubt, you walk deeper into truth.

Even as they try their hardest to give it, we can recognize rubbish when it's coming our way. That garbage may come out of a place of caring that has morphed into controlling behavior. Maybe the trash givers don't have the skills needed to nurture a relationship. Perhaps they are as broken and shattered as can be because they carry their own burdens accumulated from the past.

Whatever the reason, the trash is not yours to receive.

We find rest as we transition spiritually and emotionally from "Thank you for this trash" to "This is not my trash."

We find refuge as we are open to honest critique and loving and constructive conversations. But a heaping dish of gross old trash is not for us.

Our identity comes from a Savior who loved us from the beginning and loves us still.

Lord, thank you for this amazing woman who is your daughter. Your Word says she is beloved. It declares that she is made with a purpose. You take our broken pieces and make a masterpiece out of them. Sort through the rubbage and help her remove anything that doesn't belong. Help her to see herself the way you do, rather than through a broken lens. Amen.

PAUSE POINT

I've prayed for you. Now write your own prayer. Ask for rest from this burden that is heavy-laden.

_____

_____

_____

Real Life

This chapter might have left you feeling exposed. It may have brought something to the surface that you would rather not think about. You may even want to rush past it or bury it. After all, you're strong. You're doing just fine.

I hear you, friend.

We all deserve safe relationships, and God is our Rest.

That safe place isn't somewhere you hide. It's hidden in you. You don't have to change or fix anything before receiving the safe place he offers.

> **JOY STEALER**
>
> When you embrace the words of a broken person as your identity.

There's joy waiting as you bring that inner critic or bad theology or misguided ideas about God's character into his presence. Your struggle is real, but so is your relationship with Jesus—and it's greater.

Nothing can take your joy away, because no one can take your Jesus away.

JoyKeeper:

Exchange Your Labor and Heavy Burden for Rest

Truth

The righteous will rejoice in the Lord and take refuge in him; all the upright in heart will glory in him.—Psalm 64:10

Live It

- Recognize anything that tries to steer you away from the safe place Jesus offers.
- If your inner critic says you are unlovable or unworthy, bring that story to God.
- Put it down as often as you need until it stays down.

When anyone or anything tries to tell you that God doesn't love you or you are not worthy of his love, refute it with the Word. The Bible calls this our belt of truth. When that voice is loud and disruptive, read Romans 8:38–39. Put your name in the verse. Let the truth of how much God loves you soak over your heart and bring you rest.

Jesus, thank you for the rest you offer. If I have misguided beliefs about you, expose them. If there are wounded places you want to heal further, I give you total access. You are my safe place. There's no one who can take your place. In Jesus's name, amen.

five

you are not shame

The correctional facility is located on a busy main street. The building is nondescript, almost hidden away. There's nothing on the outside to indicate 130-plus women are housed behind bars for offenses ranging from drug possession to more aggressive crimes.

When I was asked to speak, I said yes immediately. This would be my second time.

The first time I watched as over one hundred women, wearing facility-issued yellow clothing, walked through the door. They held their hands behind their backs as a safety policy. I also observed Rita, a vibrant seventy-one-year-old faith warrior, as she and her team taught and loved these women.

While they can't physically touch them, that doesn't keep their fingerprints of love off of them. When they pray, they place their hands in the air over their shoulders, words pouring over them. When a woman completes her time at the correctional facility, the team connects her with resources, such as gently used high-quality clothing so she can find a job, as well as with a faith community as she starts her new life.

As I prepped the message, I longed to love them well, just as Rita and her team had modeled. I asked God for a fresh word for these women.

He knows each of them by name.

He knows the plans he has for them.

I believed he had a word specifically for them.

And he did. Yet the moment the word slipped into my heart, I wanted to give it back. This particular message would tiptoe into raw areas, and I felt unqualified to speak it.

I knelt and asked again, "Are you sure, Lord?"

Yes, this was the message I was supposed to share.

A few nights later I stood in front of my sisters dressed in yellow.

I wish you had been there, friend.

I wish you could have felt the presence of the Holy Spirit in that room. I wish you were standing next to me to witness unholy chains falling off. There are moments in ministry I'll never forget, and this is one of them. When the meeting was over, I walked past barred doors and down concrete hallways, tears streaming down my cheeks.

The message I struggled to share fell into barren places, and life sprung out of hungry soil.

The message I shared that night isn't just for the beautiful women in the correctional facility. It's for me. It's for you. It's for all of us, and this is what the Holy Spirit asked me to say:

You are not shame.

You and I were never meant to be defined by shame.

Our futures are not dictated by shame.

We are not denied access to God's love because of shame.

Shame is a major joy stealer.

Shame is a bully, and we don't have to be behind bars to be imprisoned by it.

Truth #5: God's goodness is greater.

WHAT I FEEL: I am bad.

WHAT I KNOW: God's goodness is greater.

It wasn't so long ago that you were mired in that old stagnant life of sin. You let the world, which doesn't know the first thing about living, tell you how to live. You filled your lungs with polluted unbelief, and then exhaled disobedience. We all did it, all of us doing what we felt like doing, when we felt like doing it, all of us in the same boat. It's a wonder God didn't lose his temper and do away with the whole lot of us. Instead, immense in mercy and with an incredible love, he embraced us. He took our sin-dead lives and made us alive in Christ.—Ephesians 2:1–5 MESSAGE

Shame is different from healthy regret or conviction, both of which can lead to transformation. It's far deeper than a critical voice that we battle from time to time. Instead, shame weaves itself into your identity. It demands you interact with the world as if your past sins, whether ten years or ten minutes ago, are who you are and who you are always going to be.

Shame tells you didn't do something bad, you *are* bad.

This creates a shame sequence in which too many of God's daughters are held captive. It works something like this:

We sin

↓

Shame says we are bad

↓

which leads to secret-keeping, isolation, and mask-wearing

↓

which causes us to feel stuck

↓

which tempts us to give up or to give in to that sin or sin identity

↓

reinforcing the message that we are bad/too far gone/shameful

A shame sequence is a dark pit in which the enemy of our souls longs to keep us, trying to oppose the truth that Jesus conquered sin once and for all.

What a Shame Culture Teaches Us

As I prepped my message for the women in the correctional facility, I read a passage I had marked earlier in the week, Ephesians 2:1–10. Three important questions surfaced as I studied this deeper.

1. When did Jesus love us?
2. How does Jesus love us?
3. Why did Jesus love us?

These are core questions of our faith. The answers have the power to shut down a shame sequence. But what if you are stuck in a pit of shame? You might not know how to answer these questions when your faith, your relationship with God, and your perception of his love are viewed through that pit.

Knowing if your belief system is skewed by shame is important. Let's pause for a moment. Answer the three questions for yourself. Don't try to offer a "right" answer or what you think someone wants you to say. Just share what you truly believe.

1. When did Jesus love you?

_____

_____

_____

2. How does Jesus love you?

3. Why did Jesus love you?

Paul wrote four letters, one of them the book of Ephesians, while in prison. He had spent almost three years in the city of Ephesus building a thriving church. One day he made a wealthy businessman angry. There were so many converts that the silversmith's business suffered. Evidently people were less interested in buying idols than in the teachings of Jesus, and that was costing the businessman money. The man started a riot and Paul was put under house arrest.

In the first chapter of Ephesians, Paul reminds his friends of the gifts Jesus gave—hope, power, love, his life, his death, and his resurrection. He assures them that all of these influence who they are. Then Paul reminds them of what they were when that gift was offered; they were spiritually dead.

> And you were dead in the trespasses and sins in which you once walked, following the course of this world, following the prince of the power of the air, the spirit that is now at work in the sons of disobedience—among whom we all once lived in the passions of our flesh, carrying out the desires of the body and the mind, and were by nature children of wrath, like the rest of mankind.—Ephesians 2:1–3 ESV

At this point, Paul's words are oh-so-familiar to his friends.

Words like *disobedience, trespasses, sins,* and *wrath* were things they had heard their whole lives. This audience was raised (and lived) in a shame-and-honor culture. They learned, from a young age, a very specific definition of honor and also the control of shame. It worked like this: If you lived an honorable life, you and your family were publicly viewed as good, moral, decent, and worthy.

If, however, you did something shameful, or you *were* something shameful, not only did you lose your honor, but your family hung their heads. Shame and honor were powerful ways to keep you in line. The emphasis was on behavior and appearances. Of course, the desire was to live a holy life behind the scenes, but your personal worth as a human being was tied to public respect for you.

The price of dishonor was costly. If you brought shame on your family, you were rejected or shunned in order for them to regain their status among neighbors, authority, and the community.

The recipients of the letter had no idea that Paul was about to add a sweet holy twist to the topic of shame.

A Culture of Shoulds and Don'ts

While a patriarchal shame-and-honor culture thrives in countries even today, it's not as obvious in the Western world. It presents itself in a subtler form, even in our faith culture, in the form of a list of shoulds and don'ts such as these:

- Don't look at that.
- Don't touch that.
- Don't be that.
- Don't be with that person/people group.
- You should be more like me/her/us.
- You should act more like me/her/us.

While this is a short list of shoulds and don'ts, you most likely have a list simmering in your brain. In most cases, the people teaching you this method sincerely love you. It's shame based, but also fear based. They want to keep you away from things that could harm you. They want you to have a "good" life. They want you to represent well.

Perhaps they don't want you to make the same mistakes they did.

We can also adopt shame and honor as a method to keep ourselves in check. If we adhere to all the shoulds and don'ts on our list, we are "good."

If we tell ourselves how bad we are, how bad things will be if we keep doing what we are doing, or how dangerous that thing is, maybe we'll stop or never do it in the first place. When we do those things, we mentally shift from the good category to the bad.

Can you see the glaring gaps in the shoulds and don'ts, especially if they're wrapped around faith? It all hinges on our own efforts.

Not too long ago, a woman recognized me in an airport and asked if we could talk. I had several minutes before my flight was to depart, so we settled in for a chat.

She told me how things were unraveling in her life. "I don't understand," she said. "I did everything I was supposed to." Then she listed all the things. The shoulds, the don'ts. She checked them all off the list. She lived a "good" life just as she was taught. She truly was a good person at heart. Her desire was to please God and do the right thing.

"Then why didn't it work out for me?" she asked.

When we live by the shame-and-honor culture (or the shoulds and don'ts), the message we receive is that when we are "good," we will be rewarded. Our kids will follow Jesus. Our marriage will not struggle. Things will work out.

Yet when we read the Bible, it's clear that Jesus's followers faced deceitful and hurtful humans. They went to prison unjustly. They had to work through conflict with a brother or sister in Christ. Sometimes they were misunderstood, tired, or in a hard season. The undercurrent of joy threading through their lives was not their goodness or how good their lives were, but the deeper reality of God's goodness.

Jesus was sent because a lengthy list of shoulds and don'ts never worked for God's people. It created distance rather than intimacy. It supported systems where man piled on additional rules and regulations out of a sincere desire to live a holy life. It set up a belief that being "good" was the ultimate prize—instead of the joy of knowing God and being known by him no matter how easy or challenging the circumstances of the moment are.

A Fresh Word

Paul has just described our sinful nature to the church of Ephesus, but then he shares a fresh word. One that doesn't make sense to his listeners at all.

> But God, being rich in mercy, because of the great love with which he loved us, even when we were dead in our trespasses, made us alive together with Christ—by grace you have been saved—and raised us up with him and seated us with him in the heavenly places in Christ Jesus, so that in the coming ages he might show the immeasurable riches of his grace in kindness toward us in Christ Jesus.—Ephesians 2:4–7 ESV

These are startling words in a shame-and-honor culture—a culture that deems you unclean, unworthy, and unwanted by your own family when you mess up.

I wonder how many of the Ephesians pondered these words throughout the night, and the next few days, hoping and praying that they were true.

God loved us, even while we were dead in our sins and trespasses.

JOY STEALER

When you depend on your goodness rather than on God's.

When I stood in front of the women in the correctional facility, I read through Ephesians 2:1–10 and we worked through the Scriptures together. Afterward, I asked a simple question.

"When did Jesus love you?"

One woman looked up, tears welling. "When I was dead in my trespasses and sins," she whispered.

I could see that these words had soaked in, working their way past all the voices that had told her she was unworthy, unloved, unclean.

"When did Jesus love you?" I asked again.

Many of the women held my gaze, faces upturned, many with tears on their cheeks. "When I was dead in my trespasses and sins." The words rose.

"When did Jesus love you?" I asked a final time.

Women all over the room responded. Tears streaming. Hands raised. "When I was dead in my trespasses and sins!" they shouted.

There's a moment when Scripture transitions from teaching to truth to transformation. These women grabbed on to a truth—contrary to shame, which says Jesus can only love us when we become good, when we do the right thing, when we clean up, show up, and line up, when we stop making wrong choices, and when we gain the approval we have lost from family, friends, and those whose opinion matters.

His goodness is far greater than our shame.

Will we embrace the same message?

When we do, it completely changes the shame sequence from "You are bad" to a message of hope. It looks like this:

You sin. → He loved you while you were yet in your sin.

Shame says you are bad → His goodness is greater.

↓

which leads to transparency, seeking help, and truth-telling

↓

which leads to healing and hope

↓

which reveals your true identity

↓

which draws you closer to Christ and a new beginning

↓

which unfolds his goodness in your life

If you explore generations of a shame-and-honor culture, you'll find it simply cleans up the outside. It doesn't touch the inside, where God does his greatest work. By expressing his love for us while we are yet dead in our sins and trespasses, he throat-punches the enemy's plans to steal, kill, and destroy us.

- Instead of hiding or secret keeping, we go to the Light to find the grace we need.
- We seek the cleansing he offers.
- We ask for the forgiveness we need and the courage to begin fresh.
- We leave behind shame to embrace transparency with ourselves, with others, and with God.

There will be work to do, but that's okay. He'll help us with that too. As we do, shame transitions to conviction and we leave behind snarled roads we were never meant to travel. With his help we do the hard work of reconciliation and consequences, all the while knowing we are loved. All the while understanding that God's plan will continue to unfold as we walk with him.

Let's answer this question a second time.

PAUSE POINT

When did Jesus love you?

_____

_____

Did your answer change? Explain why.

_____

_____

How Does Jesus Love Us?

Months after my son's journey out of addiction, he invited his dad to take a trip overseas.

Two pastors and five men, including my son and my husband, traveled to a sister church to meet with men in a recovery house. The house was located in a country dominated by a shame-and-honor culture. Each day they met with men of all ages. Several of the men told their stories. Part of those stories was that they brought shame to their families when they sought help for their addictions.

It was a lose-lose situation. Their addictions brought personal shame. Seeking help brought public shame to them and their families. Several were rejected because of it.

It was Ryan's first time to publicly share his story.

When he told the men of his dad's reaction the night he called us, the men were stunned. Several of the men approached Richard afterward. He listened as they spoke the words they couldn't tell their own fathers. Forehead to forehead, Richard prayed and wept with them.

How did Jesus love us?

Paul answers this second question beautifully.

God loved us with a father's love.

> And God raised us up with Christ and seated us with him in the heavenly realms in Christ Jesus, in order that in the coming ages he might show the incomparable riches of his grace, expressed in his kindness to us in Christ Jesus.—Ephesians 2:6–7

He lifts us up. Not just out of the pit of shame and sin, but into heavenly realms, right by his own Son. Only he can do this. This elevates us from lost to found. From alienated to embraced. From a fallen identity to child of God, but also an heir. By doing so, he reveals the unrivaled riches of his grace. God's love was and is kind. It brings life to our dormant places as he sweeps over them with mercy. This is a gift. It's not our own doing. It's not the result of following a list of shoulds and don'ts. "For it is by grace you have been saved, through faith—and this is not from yourselves, it is the gift of God—not by works, so that no one can boast" (Ephesians 2:8).

When we accept this gift, we move from believing we are bad to shunning shame. We don't accept the label. We don't allow it to define us. When it crosses our path (and it will), we reject it and move away from it, toward grace.

Toward love.

Toward a heavenly Father who is kind, who sees you as his daughter, who has lifted you out of shame to be exactly who you were always meant to be.

Most importantly, we stop trying to make ourselves lovable to God when he already loves us.

As we do this, shame is stripped of its power.

PAUSE POINT

Take a moment and speak to shame. Remind shame who you are.

_____

_____

_____

Why Did Jesus Love Us?

God didn't offer grace to merely save our lives. He offered grace to make something beautiful from it. "For we are his workmanship, created in Christ Jesus for good works, which God prepared beforehand, that we should walk in them" (Ephesians 2:10 ESV).

You are his workmanship. Many Bible translations say you are his masterpiece. The Greek word behind this is *poiema*, which means "beautiful poem" or "work of art."

There are women who grow up believing they are bad. The shame they carry isn't from their own actions, but another's sin against them. In my book *The Mended Heart*, I shared how God can heal us. It's a beautiful and intricate healing.

> *JoyKeeper*
> You stop trying to make yourself lovable to God— when he already loves you.

> Our heart mends as our inner self—the central or innermost part of our identity—is wrapped around the Light inside of us, rather than around the people who have harmed us.[1]

When Jesus conquered sin, he carried the sins of the world on him. Not just the sin itself, but the sorrow of sin inflicted on a world his heavenly Father loved.

Why did Jesus love us?

Because he knew who we were meant to be from the beginning. He confronted the power of sin and the enemy who pursues us and lies to us. As we heal, we become an integral part of an army of warrior women who walk with Jesus. We aren't afraid to say, "Me too," or, "I was there," or, "That was me."

Our shame stories become our healing stories as we come alongside others who long for freedom too.

We are all needed in this plan.

The once broken. The one rescued from her sin.

The good and those who once felt "bad."

Sharing the miracle that God is performing has the power to set others free. It's one of the most beautiful steps we can take in faith—even as God continues his work in us.

---

1. Suzanne Eller, *The Mended Heart: God's Healing for Your Broken Places* (Grand Rapids, MI: Revell, 2014), 48.

Real Life

Years earlier she sinned. It was public knowledge.

That sin cost her almost everything. After she and God began the healing process, there was hard work ahead. She went to counseling. She began to rebuild trust with her husband, children, close friends, and extended family. But her ongoing healing didn't stop judgment from following her. Judgment showed up in the grocery store. It attended her children's events. Though there were many cheering her on, sometimes judgment sat down the pew from her.

She had a choice, and it wasn't easy.

Accept the judgment as the final word, or believe that God would process her story.

Shame isn't a respecter of persons or sins or mistakes, or even of sins of others that have marked you. It's simply a seeker of vulnerability, poised to inject its poison just as you take a leap of faith. Just when God is trying to shine a spotlight on who you are becoming, or demonstrate his love through you, shame desires to swoop in to rob that moment.

Shame longs to silence the body of Christ. It will try to tell you that your past mistakes (whether five years or five minutes ago) ring louder than God's present victories.

When people were healed of obvious ailments in Scripture—ailments that people could see, like leprosy—Jesus sent them to the temple to see the priest.

Communities were tight-knit. Everyone knew about the leper. That person, though his or her skin was now as new as a baby's bottom, could expect rejection as he or she approached the priest, who would examine the leper's new skin, perhaps at first in disbelief.

JOY STEALER

Defining yourself by your backstory instead of your "But God" story.

Is this real?

Is this a temporary healing?

102

Is there disease hiding where no one can see?

As we shun shame and embrace new life, there's a good chance some will challenge whether it's real or temporary. They may bring up your past. They may scrutinize your life, which is challenging when you are re-learning and rediscovering what it is to live in relationship with God rather than in shame. They may withhold trust until you pass a certain point.

JoyKeeper

Your new story isn't something you earn. It's something you are becoming.

None of this tarnishes the miracle taking place in you.

Paul described himself as the chief of sinners (1 Timothy 1:15 NKJV). He described how he pursued believers. He put innocent people in prison and terrorized their families. He always followed this with his "But God," story. "But God, being rich in mercy, because of the great love with which he loved us, even when we were dead in our trespasses, made us alive together with Christ" (Ephesians 2:4–5 ESV).

Which of Paul's stories do we remember when we think of him? We know his backstory, but he is known by the second season of his life. We read his words and learn from them. We are drawn closer to Jesus because of the work Jesus did in him.

As God does a work in you, you may be judged.

Others can decide whether to receive your new story or not, but they aren't in charge of processing your story. That's something you and God will do over time.

Who will you allow to process your story?

Is it another person, or is it Jesus?

Is it judgment, or is it Jesus?

When the voice of judgment tries to convince us that we went too far, that God can't use us, we remind him that

Jesus loves us . . .
not because of works or how worthy we are,
but through his grace and overwhelming mercy.

Jesus died . . .
to help us find life again.

Jesus rose . . .
and we are forever changed as we receive this great gift.

Our new story isn't something we earned. It's something we are becoming.

JoyKeeper:
You Are Defined by a New Story

Truth

You're no longer strangers or outsiders. You *belong* here, with as much right to the name Christian as anyone. God is building a home. He's using us all—irrespective of how we got here—in what he is building. He used the apostles and prophets for the foundation. Now he's using you, fitting you in brick by brick, stone by stone, with Christ Jesus as the cornerstone that holds all the parts together. We see it taking shape day after day—a holy temple built by God, all of us built into it, a temple in which God is quite at home.—Ephesians 2:19–22 MESSAGE

Live It

When shame tries to tell you that you are bad, remind it that . . .

His *Goodness* is greater.

He *Redeems* what the enemy meant for harm.

He took *All* sin upon himself.

And he *Conquered* it.

His forgiveness *Extends* as far as the east is from the west.

Jesus, take this shame sequence I've been living and rewrite it with your love. In Jesus's name, amen.

six

take your seat

Picture God coming to you and saying, "Take your place at the table, sis."

He asks you to use that gifting. Step into that circle. Run after that dream or calling or his plan for you. He asks you to live with a confident heart.

What is your response?

I asked this of a handful of women. Some responded with enthusiasm. *Bring it!* Others shared the anxiousness that accompanies an invitation like this.

What if I'm not ready?

What if I don't fit in at that table?

What if I mess up in front of everybody?

The last table hurt me, so no thank you.

I'm not sure what is expected of me.

I understand these replies, because I've wrestled with them.

Taking our place at the table begins when we realize there is a seat just for us.

It's not an accident. It's part of a plan. The table is wide and long and deep, and there's more than enough room for all of us. It's filled with women who love Jesus. These women are at all stages in their relationship with him. They arrive with different backgrounds and experiences. They bring an eclectic swath of talents and personalities with them. They are all tongues, tribes, and nations. When we take our seat at the table, it produces an army of faith-filled women.

When these women stand together in Jesus's name, the world is changed.

This may sound oversimplified, but consider this—the enemy of our soul fights against it with everything he's got.

He begins by spinning a lie that you and I don't have a place at the table. This lie causes us to stand outside the door. We worry that this table isn't for us. It may cause us to try too hard or to walk away completely.

This lie tells women that if we are our real selves with other women, we'll be rejected. This lie tells us that we are too quiet. Too loud. Too creative. Too ill-equipped. Too late. Too early. Too old. Too young. Too *something* to have a seat at the table.

This lie is a colossal joy stealer.

Truth #6: God has a seat for you.

. . . .

WHAT I FEEL: I should be like her.
WHAT I KNOW: God has a seat for me.

I looked again. I saw a huge crowd, too huge to count. Everyone was there—all nations and tribes, all races and languages. And they were *standing*, dressed in white robes and waving palm branches, standing before the Throne and the Lamb and heartily singing:

> Salvation to our God on his Throne!
> Salvation to the Lamb! —Revelation 7:9–10 MESSAGE

. . . .

I'm a fighter at heart. That's surprising for some, but not to God.

It was an all-night shift at a large retail store. I worked there every weekend while attending a two-year college. It was one of two jobs that helped me stay in school. There were only a handful of employees in the entire building that night. A man came in with a woman at his side. Her eyes were red-rimmed. Her hair a mess. She wasn't wearing the right amount of clothing for the chilly night. They took almost an hour going through the store, and when they came to the register, I noticed price tags had been switched. There were several large-ticket items with ridiculously low prices. I called for a price check, hoping a manager (or anybody) would respond.

The guy stared at me. "The price is right there," he says, jabbing his finger.

"Let's go," the woman said.

He had her by the arm. Dark bruises scattered up and down her flesh. I called for a price check a second time, my voice a little more urgent. She tried to pull away, and he grabbed her and yanked her closer. As the manager approached, they abandoned the cart and ran outside.

I was explaining the situation to the manager when I heard shouting. The couple stood just outside the front door. He shoved her. I left the conversation with my manager midsentence and ran to the front door.

"Are you okay?" I asked.

I told her I'd call the police for her. I asked her to come inside where it was warm. I glared at the guy, putting every bit of my skinny eighteen-year-old frame into the stare.

He stalked away, leaving her behind.

As an adult, I realize how foolish I was. I threw myself into a skirmish that could have gone all kinds of wrong. I should have called the police rather than run to the front door. Time has sprinkled wisdom and discernment in my approach, but I'm still a fighter. I cannot look away when the odds are stacked against a

woman or child. I'm not naïve enough to think I'm anyone's rescuer or fixer, but I believe God sees that fighting spirit as a positive,
when it's used for his purposes and by his leading.

God Put Us Together

In 1 Corinthians 12, Paul compares the body of Christ to a human
body. He shares how varied we all are. Some are front and center.
Others behind the scenes. Some lead. Others serve. He compares
us to hands. Feet. Nose. Eyes. Digestive system.
Yes, even that.
I love the image portrayed in *The Message*—I lauged out loud
the first time I read it. It's so vivid!

> But I also want you to think about how this keeps your significance
> from getting blown up into self-importance. For no matter how
> significant you are, it is only because of what you are a part of. An
> enormous eye or a gigantic hand wouldn't be a body, but a monster.
> What we have is one body with many parts, each its proper size
> and in its proper place. No part is important on its own. Can you
> imagine Eye telling Hand, "Get lost; I don't need you"? Or, Head
> telling Foot, "You're fired; your job has been phased out"? As a
> matter of fact, in practice it works the other way—the "lower" the
> part, the more basic, and therefore necessary. You can live without
> an eye, for instance, but not without a stomach. When it's a part
> of your own body you are con-
> cerned with, it makes no differ-
> ence whether the part is visible
> or clothed, higher or lower. You
> give it dignity and honor just
> as it is, without comparisons.
> If anything, you have more con-
> cern for the lower parts than the
> higher. If you had to choose, wouldn't you prefer good digestion
> to full-bodied hair?—1 Corinthians 12:19–24

JOY STEALER

When you disqualify
yourself from taking a
seat, even as Jesus in-
vites you to take it.

Just as he created our physical bodies with elaborate detail, the plan for the body of Christ is just as beautiful. Which is why it's such a travesty when we chop off a hand or poke out an eye because it doesn't conform to our expectations.

It's just as tragic when we apply a set of strikes to ourselves.

God put the body together (v. 24). So let's stop to have a conversation with him. He's the one who made you. He's the one who made that one sitting across from or next to you.

He's the one who knows what can happen when we all take our seat.

PAUSE POINT

If God came to you today and said, "Sis, take your seat. It's waiting just for you," what would you say in response?

_____

_____

_____

Your answer may reflect your concerns, and that's honest. It's a great place to begin. When they are written in black and white, they aren't hidden. We see where the struggle lies.

Let's go a little bit deeper.

PAUSE POINT

Describe one trait or gifting of yours that you believe God has used to help others. This doesn't have to be big. It doesn't have to be public. Perhaps people come to you for this particular thing. Maybe you felt God nudge you to do it, and it made a difference. Whatever it is, write it down.

_____

_____

_____

There's Joy in Purpose

After the resurrection, Jesus spends time with the disciples for a few glorious weeks. When it is time to go back to the Father, he huddles with them and prays. This prayer is stunning in its intimacy (see John 17:6–19).

Jesus tells his Father that he has walked closely with the disciples. He tells him how they brought glory to him. He requests protection over them. He asks for unity among them. He prays they will live with a measure of *his* joy within them (v. 13).

These men and women have left behind old identities and marched into new territory. It took time, but eventually they understood they were part of a grand mission. Some followed Jesus out of sheer curiosity but came to firmly believe he was the Messiah.

Their relationship with Jesus took them far from their own plans and dreams. It launched them out of the comfortable. Yet there was joy as they united with him and his plans and found purpose.

Purpose is defined as "the reason for which something is created."

As they walked with Jesus, this unfolded.

Years later, when John was an old, old man, he tried his best to explain it. He had experienced a relationship with Jesus. He saw his miracles and sat under his teaching. This led John to teach and lead others. He became a respected elder in the Christian movement. Most of his friends had died a martyr's death as a result of their belief in Christ, and John wept tears over those losses. He was persecuted, confined in the wilderness, and boiled in oil.

It's hard to imagine, yet here he was at the end of his life, and he couldn't help but repeat the words Jesus spoke over him so many years ago.

> We proclaim to you what we have seen and heard, so that you also may have fellowship with us. And this fellowship of ours is with the Father and with His Son, Jesus Christ. We write these things so *that our joy may be complete.*—1 John 1:3–4 BSB, emphasis added

John found his seat! He became a part of the plan. There are a thousand distractions that cause us to forget why we call ourselves believers. We can become hyperfocused on things that carry little weight in eternity.

PAUSE POINT

What might happen if we kept our focus on the plan?

_____

_____

_____

God created you to be you

↓

We come together in his name

↓

The world is changed as a result

↓

Purpose = Joy

John didn't equate joy with a list of his accomplishments, which by this time was lengthy. He didn't offer numbers—how many people, how large a region, how many churches he had established. He was created to fellowship with Jesus and with others.

He lived with a measure of joy within as a result.

This is how we explain believers, chained and in a dark and dangerous prison, singing at the top of their lungs. This is how we explain a church working through conflicts and differences while still changing their community and the world. This is how we explain people giving up comfort and material goods to create greater community.

They put value on community and unity. They saw them as mutual.

As they found their seats, they held out a seat for the person next to them, and there was more joy.

As they led people a little closer to Jesus, they watched with joy as their eyes were opened to his love.

God created us with a purpose.

God put us together for a purpose.

So what gets in our way?

We Aren't Sure What to Do

Years ago, the Holy Spirit let me in on a little secret.

It's not what you do that delights God. It's who you are.

That seemed impossible. I was such a mess. There was so much to learn.

Then I matured in my faith. Doors were opened. I transitioned from someone who was asking all the questions to someone who had an answer now and then.

Once again, the Holy Spirit reminded me of that little secret.

Suzie, it's not what you do that delights God. It's who you are.

You and I were created to know him.

That's our purpose.

Worship flows out of that. Works (not a to-do list, but where he leads) flow out of that. Direction flows out of that. His plans—so much greater than our own—flow out of that.

Let's be honest, though.

When he leads us to something new or different, we'd like to know what to do.

JoyKeeper

It's not what you do that delights God. It's who you are.

Studying the Bible was once new territory for me. Leading a Bible study? Same thing. Being a mom. Stepping into confidence. Speaking. Opening my home to others. All of this was new.

Very few of us know exactly what to do in the beginning.

In fact, once we figure it out, there's usually a new adventure right around the corner.

We learn what to do *as* we do it.

I'm a better mom now than I was when my kids were little. There were so many things I didn't know. It often felt like trial and error. If I were to give myself a grade, I was high on play and love and low in other practical areas, but I grew as I parented. My role has shifted and changed, and I'm still learning and growing as a mom, mother-in-law, and Gaga.

The first time I led a Bible study, I overprepared and syphoned all the fun out of it. That study was for eight people, and I was as anxious as if I had been standing in front of hundreds of people.

Years later, when I did stand in front of hundreds of people, I realized how instrumental those first steps were. They weren't stepping-stones to something bigger, that's not what I'm saying at all. Those small groups were exactly where God wanted me. He taught me how to relax, how to have fun, how to share the Word and unpack it. He taught me to give myself grace when it didn't go as well as I hoped (that will happen). He revealed I had the heart of a teacher and encourager, and that he could use those gifts no matter the size of the crowd.

I still teach a small group in my home. It matters as much as what I do on the stage.

When we don't know what to do, we begin where we are. We accept the fact that there are things we won't know, and that's normal. We say yes to opportunities as they come our way, even if they make our heart beat faster.

We understand that we'll make mistakes and won't die as a result.

If you feel God asking you to encourage women, look at the women right in front of you. You might start a study over coffee with a friend or invite a handful of neighbors around your kitchen table. If you sense God asking you to be an advocate for children, look for volunteer opportunities and training in your church or community.

Recently I was challenged to do something new.

It was a gentle nudge that wouldn't go away. There is incredible hurt in our nation due to prejudice. I'm grieved by it, but I'm not big enough to fix it. When I looked at what was right in front of me, I decided I could open my home to new friends from diverse cultures.

When we get together, we prepare different cultural recipes that are delicious. We hang out and laugh and talk and get to know each other; we pray.

Consider one thing you feel God asking you to do right now.

It might be as general as making a new friend. It could be something he's been asking you to do for a long time.

PAUSE POINT

What are the opportunities right where you are? Jot down all the possibilities that come to mind. (It's okay to do this with a couple of friends. In fact, it's fun.) As you do this, let all the pressure go.

_____

_____

_____

You are connected with him. He connects you with others. It's all part of the plan. There's joy in that. Give yourself room to learn what to do as you do it.

Community Is Messy

You might struggle to take your place at the table because community is messy.

You know what? You are right. It is messy.

If we factor that in from the start, we aren't surprised by it. It's messy because people are involved (including me and you). Even the most well-planned, best-implemented communities will come with a side of messy.

There are benefits in the midst of messy.

JoyKeeper

You understand that community might be messy, because you are a little messy too.

Community helps us live our faith outside a bubble. We wrestle with Scripture and dig deep into what we believe with others who might see it a little differently. We find commonality. We offer grace where we differ.

We learn to work through conflict. I've not been in any type of community that had zero conflict. Not too long ago Richard and I were with another couple. We were chatting, and suddenly the conversation fell into awkward territory. This was rare because these are long-time friends, but we saw things differently on an issue.

In the end, we simply didn't see it the same way. We are not clones. We won't all think alike, and it's unreasonable to think we should. The fact that we disagree on an issue doesn't mean it's time to close the door. It's an opportunity to try to understand where they are coming from. It's an opportunity to be gentle rather than confrontational.

If a community is toxic, shake the dust and keep going. That's biblical.

But messy? That comes with being human, even when we love Jesus.

Another benefit of community is we aren't fighting alone. Community shows up when we are in a crisis. We show up when they are in that hard place.

Every community has strengths and also weaknesses. That's where grace comes in. When we are hurt, we work through it and forgive, but there's a second step just as important.

We don't shut down all community. This is another con job of the enemy. The intent is isolation. It's his desire to divide. Isolate. Strip joy from God's people.

Somehow, God uses messy community to draw people to him.

When I realize that community will be messy, I don't come to it as if I'm not messy too. You'll get glimpses of my flaws and strengths and goofiness—the whole me. I realize I'm surrounded by women who are just as vulnerable, just as strong, just as human, and just as flawed as I am. When I mess up, I'll apologize. She doesn't have to receive it, but I'll mean it. It's important that I offer it.

> JOY STEALER
>
> When you wait for the perfect church or community.

Using the word *tribe* makes me feel silly, but I believe belonging to one is one of the most joy-filled things we can do.

Real Life

Imagine standing outside a circle. Women are leaning in. Attentive to each other. It's like they all are sharing the same secret.

You want to be in that circle, but can you?

To the ultraconfident woman, this might not even make sense, but it does to that woman sitting next to you (who looks ultraconfident).

For many women, the thought of breaking through a circle to find her place . . . *Well, forget that.*

The need to belong is something most of us experience.

I went to the same church for years. When we moved, I suddenly understood what it felt like to be on the outside. People weren't trying to keep me out, but it was a new community and a new church.

I had taken for granted all the things that made home feel like home.

I wasn't that shy girl who once stood at a distance. I hadn't been that girl for a long time. But it gave me a taste of how hard it is to be on the outside. It took a couple of years to put down new roots.

Taking our seat is faith-changing, but it doesn't stop there. We become circle-breakers for others. We do that as we . . .

- notice that woman standing outside the circle
- intentionally include her
- give her our spot if necessary

It doesn't take a lot to notice her.

When you walk into that space, glance around the room. You'll see her. That was me when we moved. Spiritually, I knew that I had a seat, but in this new environment, I didn't know where to go or what was available. I didn't know a single person's name. I could figure it out on my own, but a smile and a friendly face was so welcome.

When we become circle-breakers, we don't just show someone that there's a seat, we pull the seat out for her.

My friend Jennifer likes to take it a step further.

"Suzie, if it looks like there's not a seat, I'll give her mine." This came out of years of breaking into circles. Her true seat was in her faith, and she found joy in giving up her physical seat if it made someone else feel at home.

One day when we stand around the throne, we'll see all the women seated around that table. Such color. Such diversity. Such beauty! We'll raise our hands in worship and delight in the army of women we were privileged to serve with—whether we knew their names or not, whether they lived across the globe or across the street.

What a joyful experience that will be!

JoyKeeper: When You Take Your Seat, Pull One Out for Someone Else

Truth

Just as a body, though one, has many parts, but all its many parts form one body, so it is with Christ. For we were all baptized by one Spirit so as to form one body—whether Jews or Gentiles, slave or free—and we were all given the one Spirit to drink. Even so the body is not made up of one part but of many.—1 Corinthians 12:12–14

Live It

Our greatest belonging is in God's love. That's freely given and sincere. When we receive that, it gives us the courage to break the circle for others. We show her there's a seat for her.

What is a practical way to be a "circle-breaker"?

_____

_____

_____

Lord, I realize the enemy desires me to believe there is not a seat for me, or to somehow believe I am not supposed to take that seat. That's garbage! Following you is where I find my true self. As I take my seat, I'll pull out a chair for another. Together we'll partner with you to change the world with your love. In Jesus's name, amen.

part three
Living Joy

We know joy.
We keep joy.
Now we live joy.

Joy is distinctly a Christian word and a Christian thing. It is the reverse of happiness. Happiness is the result of what happens of an agreeable sort. Joy has its springs deep down inside. And that spring never runs dry, no matter what happens. Only Jesus gives that joy. He had joy, singing its music within, even under the shadow of the cross.—S. D. Gordon

seven

joy-wrapped faith

I was waiting in the driveway when Richard and the boys pulled up. My daughter and son-in-law were on a much-anticipated date. When I had last talked with Richard, the boys were in the back seat and overtired and cranky, which can happen at the end of an extra long day. It was nearly their bedtime.

They piled out of the car and gave me a brief hug.

Yep, they were exhausted.

"Hey, guys, come here," I said.

I lay on the driveway and put my hands behind my head.

"Look up."

Josiah placed his small body next to mine and wrapped an arm around my waist. Luke ran to grab a pillow and placed it next to me, then scooted close.

"What do you see?" I asked.

Like blinking Christmas lights, the stars were just appearing in the blanket of a sky.

"Do you see the Big Dipper?"

I pointed to the handle of the constellation, just starting to take shape.

For the next thirty minutes, the boys got lost in the intricacy of the universe. We found the North Star, Venus, and some obvious constellations. Then I pulled up an app on my phone that allowed us to find other constellations, and even to pinpoint the location of a satellite.

All the things that were so important earlier faded away as they stepped into the world of astronomy. We walked up and down the street in the darkness, my phone and Richard's in the boys' hands as they excitedly jumped up and down.

"Another one, Gaga!" Josiah shouted. "You won't believe this one. It's a lion!"

"I found a bear!" Luke raced toward us, his face lit up with joy.

I hoped that lying on the driveway and looking at the stars would be a nice diversion.

Instead, it opened a whole new world for them.

Joy Is More Than a Feeling. It's a Knowing.

Joy is not a white-knuckle experiment. It's not a formula. Instead, joy comes through living these truths.

Experts teach that it takes twenty-one days to develop a new way of thinking or acting. I believe it takes more time than that. Our struggles with joy didn't happen overnight. It makes sense that it might take a month, a year, or a lifetime of learning and unearthing new ways to think or be.

When I spoke with Richard on the phone that night, it was clear the boys were exhausted. They were hyperfocused on who had the most candy in their candy bag (they had just left a friend's birthday party) and who was touching whom. They are incredible little guys, but they were careening downhill on a sugar rush and a need for quiet.

I'm not six years old, and sometimes I find myself in the same place.

I'm juggling. I'm overstimulated, overtired, yet I long more than anything just to slow it all down and connect with my Source. If I continue at this pace, there's a good chance I'll get all the things done because we are good at that, right?

But I might miss what is right above me, or right inside of me, just waiting to be grasped.

In Philippians, the word *joy* is sprinkled throughout. The entire book of Philippians could be summed up in one phrase:

Take joy in your faith.

Over and over again, Paul repeats these words throughout all four chapters of his letter:

- *Rejoice* in the Lord.
- I share your *joy*.
- Whatever happens, my dear brothers and sisters, *rejoice* in the Lord.
- Always be full of *joy* in the Lord. I say it again—*rejoice!*

It doesn't make sense, not really.

Until we notice that he ties these words to another, like two halves of a perfect whole.

- I want you to *know*, my dear brothers and sisters, that everything that has happened here has helped to spread the good news.
- I want you to *know* that as you pray for me and the Spirit of Jesus Christ helps me, this will lead to my deliverance.
- I want you to *know* Christ and experience the mighty power that raised him from the dead.
- I *know* how to live on almost nothing or with everything.

If we stop and consider the marriage of these two words—*joy* and *knowing*—we see the power in them.

Real Life

A short time after I sent the manuscript for this book to my publisher, a new season of scarred began to unfold. I found out on a Thursday that my breast cancer had recurred after twenty-eight years.

The next Monday, my healthy-eating half marathon–running husband had a massive heart attack.

He went through a double-bypass open-heart surgery. As I write these words, I'm healing from a double mastectomy.

The morning after Richard's heart attack, I stumbled out of the hospital, trying to find his car. He had parked haphazardly in the emergency room parking lot, clutching his chest as he sought help.

We'd had an unusual burst of icy weather the night before, and the car door was sealed shut. I yanked at it until it finally opened. I searched for an ice scraper and couldn't find it. So I sat inside and cranked the heater up to ninety degrees, trying to melt the ice on the windows so I could move the car.

My husband was inside the hospital being prepped for a surgery we didn't see coming. I was still reeling from the news that my cancer had recurred. We were supposed to be leaving on an anniversary getaway.

What just happened?

I cried out to my heavenly Father in that ice-shrouded car.

I cried because I had cancer *again*. I wept because I couldn't find an ice scraper (it made sense at the time). I cried because I almost lost my husband. I laid my head on the steering wheel and wept because I thought the season of scarred was behind me, but here it was—back with a vengeance. I was hurting and confused and overwhelmed, but as I cried, God met me in that ice-covered Prius.

Everything in these pages held true.

Joy is more than a feeling. It's a *knowing*.

Paul's words in Philippians 3:7–8 held me close over the next several weeks. "Yes, everything else is worthless when compared with the infinite value of knowing Christ Jesus my Lord" (v. 8 NLT).

There's joy in our faith. There's value in knowing him.

A JoyKeeper becomes a joy noticer.

We start to notice what is above us and what is in us.

We begin to notice what is stronger than that hard place.

We notice who holds us close in grief.

We notice what lights us up on a really good day and know he'll still be there the next morning when it's not as easy.

We notice his goodness revealed in his people as they love us through those harder places, and even if they don't show up, he does.

We walk in the knowing until it's familiar.

This is not just a book for me. It's a journey we are all invited to take. I prayed over this book and I prayed over you. My hope is that you'll not just be inspired to live as a JoyKeeper but reach for the knowing in the nitty-gritty of everyday life.

So what's next?

Let's continue this journey together. For the next thirty days, we'll take these six truths a little deeper. Each day, we'll study one truth and then apply it to real life. You'll be tempted to push ahead, but allow each daily reading to soak in. It will be kind of like pulling on spiritual yoga pants and running shoes to start a brand-new race toward joy.

I believe in you, friend. I am excited for you.

I *know* that joy is for all of us. It may not look like what the world says it should. Rather, it's far deeper and more life-changing. Let's explore the deeper reality of God's goodness and walk with him until it feels like home.

From one JoyKeeper to another,
Suzie

devotional

thirty days to
living a joykeeper life

Day 1: His Scars

On the evening of that first day of the week, when the disciples were together, with the doors locked for fear of the Jewish leaders, Jesus came and stood among them and said, "Peace be with you!" After he said this, he showed them his hands and side. The disciples were overjoyed when they saw the Lord.—John 20:19–20

Have you ever been afraid or sad or mad and someone says, "You shouldn't feel that way"?

Well, the problem is you *do* feel that way.

Things are turning around, but there's leftover trauma that you are working through with God's help. That difficult person is still in your life or that difficult season is lingering. Yet you get up every day, determined that today will be better than yesterday. You hold on to Christ and your faith with all your being.

That makes insensitive statements that question your faith peck at your heart.

If I shouldn't feel this way, does that mean I'm failing my God, who I love so much?

God, are you disappointed with me?

I wonder if Jesus's friends thought the same. In John 20, several of Jesus's closest friends are hiding in fear. Their emotions are all over the place. They just witnessed Jesus's open tomb that very day but wonder if it is real. They are afraid of the authorities who search for them.

What will they do—these people who brutally nailed Jesus to a cross?

Jesus's friends are hopeful. They are uncertain. They are afraid. When they suddenly see a resurrected Jesus standing before them, they are stunned. He brims with glory. Then he asks them to do something unusual. He asks them to take a closer look at his scars.

Even in his glorified body, Jesus still wears the marks of battle.

By showing them his scars, he offers indisputable evidence of how hard he fought for them. By asking them to look at his side, feet, and hands, he assures them he is the same Jesus they've always known. He's their friend, but also the Son of God. Omniscient. Present.

Are you in a season that makes you feel scarred?

His healed wounds are evidence that . . .

. . . because of *his* scars, you have a relationship with him.

. . . because of *his* scars, you are free to talk to him about what is hurting your heart.

. . . because of *his* scars, he understands how you feel.

. . . because of *his* scars, he is your Healer.

You don't have to shape up or perk up to be considered strong or a faith-filled woman, because your strength is in his love for you. That strength will continue to develop as you walk with him, trusting him.

He has already won the battle for you. His scars tell the profound story that you are seen, loved, and known.

You Are a *JoyKeeper*

TRUTH: God cares about how you feel.

- Read Isaiah 53:5; John 20:19–21, 27.
- Write a letter to Jesus. Bring him up to date on how you feel.

#prayerstarter

Lord, I've carried a lie around in my heart that is as heavy as a boulder. It's a lie that says you are mad at me when I'm sad. Your scars tell the story that you know how I feel, and that you fought for me. Today I reach to feel your battle scars taken on my behalf. In Jesus's name, amen.

Day 2: Not Alone

Two people can resist an attack that would defeat one person alone.
A rope made of three cords is hard to break.—Ecclesiastes 4:12 GNT

When we feel sorrow, we may be tempted to isolate. We turn away from those who love us best. We may even shut out God.

While alone time can be helpful when feelings are tangled, we need people.

Jesus was sorrowful as the cross loomed near. He would be betrayed. Suffering was ahead. Jesus hiked to a remote location so he could pray, but he didn't go alone. He asked Peter, James, and John to stay close and keep watch while he prayed. They sleepily sat nearby while Jesus talked with his heavenly Father.

Jesus's friends didn't quite make it through the prayer session.

They were so exhausted they fell asleep. Jesus knew that in advance, but that didn't keep him from drawing them close.

Our friends may be oh-so-human as they try to love us well. Maybe they won't know what to say. Perhaps they won't know what to do. Don't let that keep you from reaching out. Don't let that keep you from sharing what you need with healthy and godly friends.

The fact that they show up means something.

Knowing they care enough to sit with us in our discomfort is a beautiful gift.

Being human is something we all understand. So we won't ask them to fix our pain or make it all go away, because only God is big enough to do that. Rather, we refuse to isolate, because connection—even in its imperfect state—makes us stronger.

While we are at it, we'll also reach for our heavenly Father, sharing our deepest needs, for he is the closest of friends.

You Are a *JoyKeeper*

TRUTH: God cares about how you feel.

- Read Ecclesiastes 4:12; Matthew 26:26–39; John 15:15.
- In what ways does reaching out make a difference?
- Reaching for help in times of sorrow is brave. If you need counsel, make that phone call.

#prayerstarter

Father, the temptation is to isolate, and that isn't your best for me. I refuse to hide from those who love me and want the best for me. They may not know what to say, and there's grace for that. We are all so human, and there have been times I haven't known what to say or do. And when people fall short, thank you that you never do. In Jesus's name, amen.

Day 3 : No More Labels

For you did not receive a spirit of slavery that returns you to fear,
but you received the Spirit of sonship, by whom we cry, "Abba!
Father!" The Spirit Himself testifies with our spirit that we are
God's children.—Romans 8:15–16 BSB

I love doing life with two close friends. One is wise and feisty. The other is compassionate and funny. Both are powerhouse women whom God uses to make a difference. Both battle with depression and anxiety.

For years they kept silent about their struggle. One day my wise and feisty friend got tired of the daily fight and went for help. Over time, she began to see life differently. My other friend addressed depression from several angles—mind, body, soul. She too began to find relief.

Their honesty about depression and anxiety opened the door for others to talk.

These two friends have taught me a powerful truth:

Depression or anxiety is not your identity. It's something you struggle with.

We all battle with something, every single one of us. When we realize this, it opens the door to talk about our very real battles with a godly friend or counselor. It removes the stigma others may place on a specific battle, or the stigma we ourselves try to place on it.

It also removes labels.

Being labeled is something we all face at one time or another. Labels put you in a box. They fail to account for the whole person. They overlook God's beautiful plan from the very beginning. Labels will always send us somewhere, and if we allow labels to become our identity, they send us down the wrong road.

You are not identified by your struggle. You are identified by your relationship with Christ. There are a hundred different words to place over your heart instead.

You are stronger than you know. You are gifted. You are an integral part of a tribe of women across the world who love Jesus. You are a difference maker.

You are deeply loved.

You Are a *JoyKeeper*

TRUTH: God cares about how you feel.

- Read Jeremiah 29:11; Romans 8:15–16; 31–39; 1 Peter 5:7.
- Write down five good things that define you—things separate from your struggle.
- If you find this difficult, ask a good friend to share one or two things about you.

#prayerstarter

Jesus, I was not created to be placed in a box, labeled by myself or by others. I am beautifully created, thoughtfully designed, built with a purpose and a plan. When someone tries to place a label on me, I will remind myself of all the things you've done in me and who I am because of you. In Jesus's name, amen.

Day 4: Trusting His Heart

My flesh and my heart may fail, but God is the strength of my heart and my portion forever.—Psalm 73:26

Trust your heart.

This is the advice people give when we don't know what to do. The problem with this advice is the heart isn't always trustworthy. The heart may respond to short-term emotion and fail to weigh long-term impact. The heart may give permission to do what we want and fail to consider the hearts of others. The heart might even lie to us to get what it wants.

In Psalm 73, the psalmist Asaph recognizes that in his own power, he is a mess.

His heart is failing him, but there's a second half to his song. He is in direct relationship with God—and all the goodness this relationship brings. His heart and flesh may fail, but God is the strength of his heart and portion forever!

You may be discouraged, but your heart and being aren't tied to circumstances or emotions alone. As a believer, you are attached with an ever-present, all-knowing, all-powerful heavenly Father. That means your heart is attached to truth, wisdom, strength, healing, and more. This demands that the messages that filter through your heart must first pass through your faith.

- You can trust he is on the scene.
- You can trust he redeems what is lost or broken.
- You can trust he will never forsake or abandon you.

As you do, you are anchored to an eternal, unmovable Source.

You Are a *JoyKeeper*

TRUTH: God cares about how you feel.

- Read Psalm 31:24; 73:26; 147:3; Ezekiel 36:26.
- Draw a heart in your journal. Write one of these verses in the center of that heart.
- What is one thing your heart is telling you to do?
- Does it align with God's? Why or why not?

#prayerstarter

I hold up my heart to you, for it is fickle right now. It does not have permission to lead me away from your best for me or those I love. As I place my trust in you, my Savior and my Lord, my heart will follow. Thank you for being my anchor in this turbulent season. In Jesus's name, amen.

Day 5: Red Light. Green Light. Yellow Light.

And the Father who knows all hearts knows what the Spirit is saying, for the Spirit pleads for us believers in harmony with God's own will.—Romans 8:27 NLT

Walking with our littles on the trail can be complicated. Bicycles race down one lane. Families, dogs, and children are in the other. Children ride scooters or skateboards. Runners race by.

Trying to keep the littles safe didn't always work until we discovered a fun game.

Red light. Green light. Yellow light.

If they race ahead or arrive at a curve or close to a busy street, I call out, "Red light!"

Regardless of how fast they are going, they stop. Yellow light means slow down. Green light means go, go, go! Making this a game made it fun, but it also made the little ones safe.

When our feelings are overwhelming, we may not know what to do.

We run in one direction or another, or we have the opposite reaction and shut down.

Then there's that limbo place where we don't know which way to turn.

Romans 8:27 reminds us that the Holy Spirit knows the heart of the Father for us in each of these situations. He knows when we should stop, go, or wait. It may be a nudge, a sense of peace, or a feeling deep inside. As we listen for his voice, we receive a red light, green light, or yellow light that helps us in that moment.

Red light: Stop, daughter. Let me help you work through that anger. It comes from a wounded place. If you react now, it will only create more wounds.

Yellow light: This isn't your assignment. Let me do the work needed. I know you can't see what I'm doing, but trust me. That's all I ask of you.

Green light: Time to go, go, go, daughter. You are brave and strong. You can do this thing. I'll show you the next step.

He knows that we wrestle with mixed feelings and that the direction is not always clear. Thankfully, he also knows what is around the corner. Inviting him into our feelings helps us to put on the brakes, take that huge leap of faith, or trust him as we wait for clear direction.

He knows where we are going and will show us the way.

You Are a *JoyKeeper*

TRUTH: God cares about how you feel.

- Read Proverbs 3:5–6; Isaiah 30:21; Jeremiah 29:11.
- When you don't know what to do, ask for wisdom. Do it often. The more you listen, the more you begin to recognize his voice.

#prayerstarter

Heavenly Father, when I have mixed feelings, you come alongside. You know what is ahead of me. Keep my feet on the path you have carved for me. In Jesus's name, amen.

Day 6: Uniquely Wired

Now you [collectively] are Christ's body, and [individually] you are members of it, each part severally and distinct [each with his own place and function].—1 Corinthians 12:27 AMPC

If you and I were sitting at a coffee shop, the first thing you'd discover is that . . . well, you'd be the only one drinking coffee. I'd be sipping a smoothie or a green something of some sort. If I drink coffee or eat anything chocolate after noon, I'll lie in bed that night, my mind racing a hundred miles an hour, my legs twitching.

For a long time I viewed this as a weakness.

If others can have chocolate or caffeine, I should be able to as well. Then I took a genetic test. As I scrolled through the results, I found this: *It's highly likely that you are sensitive to caffeine.* If this tiny detail shows up in my genes, what other traits did God so carefully place inside of me? While I'm sensitive to caffeine, I'm also an introvert. I'm attuned to people's feelings. I love to learn. I need eight hours of sleep. I'm goofy with those I love most.

God crafted us one by one.

There are no two people alike. There are no two people with the same fingerprints. Rather than compare ourselves with others, what if we embraced who God made us to be?

We'd recognize the strength of that trait. We'd also acknowledge the weakness of it.

For this caffeine-sensitive woman who needs her sleep, caffeine after noon is off limits for me, and that's okay. It doesn't matter if everyone else can chug a cup of coffee and eat that slice of chocolate cake. It's not for me. As an introvert, I have learned to show up and do my thing. I love people! But I also need to refuel shortly after.

How has God uniquely wired you?

Asking this question launches a discovery process. We explore our strengths. We discover how God uses those unique strengths to make a difference. We become aware of the weaknesses and do what is wise and best for us instead of trying to be like any other.

Most importantly, we delight in our Creator, who uniquely wired us and uniquely places us—all for a unique purpose.

You Are a *JoyKeeper*

TRUTH: God is aware of who you are becoming.

- Read Psalm 139:13–14; 1 Corinthians 8:3; 12:27–30.
- What is one unique trait God created in you?
- What is one strength of that trait?
- How has God used—or how can he use—that trait?

#prayerstarter

Like a master artist, you created me and others. This puts the spotlight not on me, but on you, and I love that. Sometimes I forget to appreciate the care you took as you wired, formed, and fashioned me. So today I want to say thank-you. In Jesus's name, amen.

Day 7: Look Up

As a face is reflected in water, so the heart reflects the real person.—Proverbs 27:19 NLT

Years ago, if I was in the store and saw you across the way, I'd go down a different aisle. It wasn't that I didn't like you or that I didn't want to be your friend; I just wasn't sure what to say.

If you spotted me first, I'd put on a good face and pretend, but afterward I'd wonder . . .

Did I say the wrong thing?

Was that as awkward as it seemed?

Today I'd put my hands on the cart and walk across the store to say hello. I wouldn't give a thought about what I said or didn't say. I'd simply enjoy the conversation with you.

Much like when looking at a reflection in the water, we can have a distorted view of who we are.

We can project that distorted image to the world. This distorted image might even tell you a big ol' lie, saying, "You'll always be this way."

Listen, no one knows you better than the One who made you.

So we look up rather than look back.

We look up rather than look down.

We look within to acknowledge how much we've grown, how far we've come, and how many miracles he's performed in this tender area.

If you've been living as if a distorted image is true, ask God to show you what he sees. You will be surprised at the beauty he longs to reveal as you ask that question. As you continue to look up, that distorted image shifts from a leading role to a minor role.

It used to define you, but now it's part of your faith story. When you stumble across someone staring at her own distorted image, you'll know what to do. You'll take her by the hand, and together, you'll look up.

You Are a *JoyKeeper*

TRUTH: God is aware of who you are becoming.

- Read Psalm 139:16–17; 2 Corinthians 5:17; Philippians 1:6.
- A byproduct of healing is that our old struggle becomes a catalyst that helps someone else overcome hers.
- Today, pray for someone who struggles in an area where God is healing (or has healed) you.

#prayerstarter

I've been looking in the wrong place, Jesus. I've allowed past words to hold me back. I've held on as if others' words are truth. No more! Peel away anything that doesn't resemble your view of who I am. I know this will take time, and you offer tons of grace in the process. Thank you in advance for the miracles to come. In Jesus's name, amen.

Day 8: A Brand-New Day

Don't worry about anything, but pray about everything. With thankful hearts offer up your prayers and requests to God. Then, because you belong to Christ Jesus, God will bless you with peace that no one can completely understand. And this peace will control the way you think and feel.—Philippians 4:6–7 CEV

t started out as a promising day, with lots of good things packed in. Until everything started going wrong. Someone got impatient. Someone else got mad. Someone's feelings were hurt. Suddenly, the good day was a mess over a bunch of little things.

Have you experienced this? I think we all have.

When this happens, and it will, it produces a lot of immediate reactions. It may even tempt us to hold on to that one bad day, and we traipse along with unsettled unforgiveness, unresolved anger, or ongoing bitterness.

One bad day doesn't have to become a bad life.

One bad moment doesn't have to produce a landslide of choices we regret later.

There will be imperfect days, and we know that going in. Someone will say the wrong thing. Someone will get on that last nerve. That might even be us, but let's not forget:

Unresolved feelings lead to longtime wounds.

Maybe that wound is in your relationship with someone you love.

Maybe that wound is in you, and you're tired of it.

Ask the Holy Spirit to help you resolve the issue—at least in your own heart. He promises to give us wisdom. This helps us measure one bad moment against a hundred really great ones with the same people. He'll lead us to mercy as we consider the times we've arrived at an event stressed and out of sorts, wearing our grouchy pants.

He reminds us to offer grace for ourselves.

He moves us away from unresolved and unhealthy paths to begin a brand new one.

You Are a *JoyKeeper*

TRUTH: God is aware of who you are becoming.

- Read Isaiah 43:18–19; 2 Corinthians 4:16–17; Philippians 4:6–7; Colossians 3:13.
- Create a map of where you want to go. Write words like *free, joyful, unburdened*, or whatever comes to mind as you pray.
- Create a second map. If there's anything taking you in the opposite direction, write those words down too. Ask God to redirect you, and cross them out, one by one.

#prayerstarter

Jesus, I've held on to these feelings for far too long. I don't want to be defined by one day or one bad moment. I choose to live every day fully. There are things you want to show me and things you long to give. I empty my heart of that one bad day to make room for the new you want to do in me. In Jesus's name, amen.

Day 9: You Are a Rock

And now I'm going to tell you who you are, really are. You are Peter, a rock. This is the rock on which I will put together my church, a church so expansive with energy that not even the gates of hell will be able to keep them out.—Matthew 16:18 MESSAGE

I held an old photo in my hands. One corner was ragged from all the years that have passed.

The girl in the photo is thin. She's shy. When that picture was taken, life was hard. She didn't know a thing about Jesus.

But Jesus knew about her.

When I look at this photo, I think of a guy named Simon. When Jesus first met him, he gave him a new name. If you were to see a photo of that moment, you might see surprise on Simon's face.

He's a good guy, but a rock? Even after he became a follower of Christ, he sometimes was less than rocklike.

Jesus saw something in Simon Peter and others did not.

Jesus knows your past. He knows what's going on in your family. He knows the stuff you are working on in your heart. He knows there are times you long to feel him close. Jesus is aware of who you are, which is amazing when we think about it!

That skinny girl in the picture? She didn't know that one day she'd write books or speak to crowds. She didn't know her worth or value. She didn't have a clue whether she could be a good mom or not.

But Jesus did.

When we trust that he sees something we do not, it changes us. It changes the direction of our lives. We hold up all the other pictures beside his view of us, and it allows for new images to be added to the collection.

Jesus knows who you are.

You may not see it yet, but that's okay. Simon didn't see it at first. Neither did I.

We learn from him day by day.

As we do, the picture changes to include the possibilities Jesus already knew.

You Are a *JoyKeeper*

TRUTH: God is aware of who you are becoming.

- Read Proverbs 3:5–6; Matthew 7:24; 16:17–19.
- The first step is to simply trust that he sees what you do not. You don't have to define that or figure it out first. It's a discovery!
- Are you excited to see yourself the way God does? Think about one reason why.

#prayerstarter

Lord, there are so many things that have influenced who I am. Some are beautiful. Some are painful. Gently peel away the outer layers to reveal your work beneath. Thank you that you see inside of me what I might not. What an adventure this will be! In Jesus's name, amen.

Day 10: Stronger Together

A person standing alone can be attacked and defeated, but two can stand back-to-back and conquer. Three are even better, for a triple-braided cord is not easily broken.—Ecclesiastes 4:12 NLT

A few years ago, I was exhausted.

I had refused to slow down—until one day it caught up with me. A friend dropped by and recognized the weight I carried, because she had been at that place too. She prayed with me. When I say prayed, I mean she called heaven down. Two people were better than one that night. A good friend was exactly what I needed. Someone who wasn't afraid to be honest. Someone who encouraged me that things would get better.

If you struggle with close friendships, you aren't alone in that.

There are a lot of reasons we struggle. When we are hurt by a friend, it might make us decide to be our own best friend. Being busy is another obstacle. When you are the new person in a city, church, or community, there are all kinds of challenges. Comparison is also a kick in the pants.

Yet if we keep potential friends at a distance, what are we missing?

In Ecclesiastes, Solomon wisely tells us that we are stronger together. There is a real enemy who desires to isolate us, for this makes us vulnerable.

When my friend dropped by, suddenly we were a three-cord braid—my friend, me, and Jesus.

Friendship may feel risky, but it's a smart risk. Sharing your faith and life with other women who love Jesus makes the journey a little bit easier. Remember these things as you reach out to a potential new friend:

- Be yourself—you have something to offer.
- Get to know that person—go beyond a first impression.
- Refuse to compare—don't compare yourself to her, or her to others. God uniquely made each of you.
- Leave lots of room for grace—there are no perfect people, including you and me.
- Lean into the friendship but lean *on* Jesus—friendship makes us stronger, but only Jesus meets our need.
- Be intentional—say hello. Reach out. Step outside your comfort zone.

You might be surprised at how a new or reconnected friendship encourages you, but you might be the friend she needed as well.

You Are a Joykeeper

TRUTH: God is aware of who you are becoming.

- Read Ecclesiastes 4:9–10; Galatians 6:2; Hebrews 10:24–25.
- Reach out to a potential new friend or an old friend.
- Set a date and a time to connect.

#prayerstarter

Lord, I am stronger with others, especially when you are at the center of the friendship. Help me to release impossible standards or to break down any walls I've built. Give me the courage to say hello. In Jesus's name, amen.

Day 11: Big Things

The master was full of praise. "Well done, my good and faithful servant."—Matthew 25:21 NLT

I read an article about women making a difference in the world. One raised funds to dig wells in villages desperate for clean water. Another started a ministry for women rescued from the slave trade. One after another, I read stories of brave women who ran with their assignments.

For a moment it caused me to look at my own life.

God, have I missed my assignment?

Is there something BIG I'm supposed to be doing?

Before the words left my mouth, I felt a gentle rebuke. I thought about the week before. One of the women who came to a Bible study at my home had shared how it was changing her. Another woman asked for prayer, and we gathered around her, seeking God with her. For a hot moment my attention almost shifted to the "bigness" of other women's assignments rather than settling into the beauty of my own.

In Matthew 25, Jesus tells the story of a man who gave his servants differing amounts of money and asked them to invest it while he was gone. When he returned, he was filled with praise for the two who had multiplied the silver entrusted to them.

But he was grieved that one man had buried the bag he had been given.

This story isn't about money. It's about the beautiful missions we are given. Mine won't look like yours. Yours won't look like your neighbor's.

My treasured assignment is to love a handful of women who meet around my table for Bible study. Sometimes it's to rock a child. At other times, it's to speak or write. That might be considered "big" in the eyes of the world, but Scripture doesn't define our assignments as big or small, because every single person impacted counts.

What is your assignment?

Whatever it is that he's trusted you to do, celebrate as a difference is made in his name.

You Are a *JoyKeeper*

TRUTH: God is God, and you are not.

- Read Matthew 25:14–30; 1 Corinthians 12:4.
- When you wake up each day, ask the Lord, "What is my assignment today?" It may be as simple as sending a text to a hurting friend.
- Whatever it is, say yes.

#prayerstarter

Jesus, I take my eyes off anyone else's assignment and I thank you for the beauty of mine. If I'm burying that assignment because of uncertainty or comparison, I release that to you. Thank you for showing me what to do and multiplying it for your sake. In Jesus's name, amen.

Day 12: Let Go

Don't fret or worry. Instead of worrying, pray. Let petitions and praises shape your worries into prayers, letting God know your concerns. —Philippians 4:6 MESSAGE

've heard the words many times. It took a while before I realized the power in them.

Let go.

I heard them as I picked up tasks that were never mine to carry. Someone was in trouble. Someone was making choices that ultimately hurt them or others. My intentions were good. I felt like I should do something. When it didn't work, it felt like failure.

What does it look like to hold on to an assignment that isn't ours?

- We try to fix someone.
- We try to change someone's attitude.
- We try to make someone believe in God when she is in an unbelieving place.
- We work hard to make people's problems go away, even when they aren't working on them at all.
- We speak words over and over, even when it's clear the other person isn't prepared to listen.

We do this because we care, but *caring* doesn't equal *assignment*. When we stop trying to fix everyone, we are freed to step into our real mission. We can pray, which is powerful and effective. If the Lord leads us to speak, we do so in love, and then allow the Holy Spirit to marinate those words at the right time. He's faithful to show us how to encourage, love, pray, believe in, or speak truth-filled words *as he leads*.

And that's the key.

Relieving yourself of an assignment that is not yours is one of the most powerful moves you can make. It invites you to love well. It allows you to fight in a whole new way as you release that one into God's capable hands.

You Are a *JoyKeeper*

TRUTH: God is God, and you are not.

- Read Psalm 46:10; Philippians 4:6.
- Read Psalm 18:16 and place your loved one's name in the Scripture.
- In the next twenty-four hours, release an assignment that is not yours.
- What might that look like?

#prayerstarter

Heavenly Father, sometimes my instinct is to rush in and make plans, especially if someone I care about has made mistakes. Show me when I start to step outside of my assignment. Give me the courage to trust you and allow you to lead the way. In Jesus's name, amen.

Day 13 : Put It Down

"Put your sword back in its place," Jesus said to him.—*Matthew 26:52*

One day I had all the words I wanted to say bubbling inside, so I grabbed my keys and headed to the front door. I was ready to go. Until I sensed that quiet voice inside . . . again.

I picked this assignment back up because when it's not working out like we hope, we want to take the wheel.

Climb on in the back seat there, Jesus.

You aren't doing this in my timing or in my way, so I'm taking over.

Regardless of how badly I wanted this assignment, it wasn't the right time.

I wasn't the right person for the job.

I leaned against my front door, tears streaming, heart surrendered. The Lord knew my words, though bathed in love, might not land like they should.

In fact, there was a good chance—because it wasn't my assignment—they'd do the opposite. I needed to allow the work of the Holy Spirit to run its course, without my interference.

Picking up assignments that aren't ours is something we all do from time to time.

Do you remember when Peter pulled out his sword in the garden of Gethsemane? Jesus told him to put away his sword. It wasn't his assignment. That probably didn't make sense to Peter as a crowd of hostile men surrounded Jesus.

Doing nothing felt wrong. Doing something, even if it was the wrong thing, felt better.

Jesus knew what Peter didn't. There was a road Jesus would travel, one that led to purpose. It was important that Peter didn't get in the way.

If you sense the Holy Spirit asking you to pick up that assignment, run with it. But if he's asked you to put one down, leave it there.

You aren't doing *nothing*. You are trusting God. You are believing. You are allowing God to take the wheel as the one he loves walks the road toward healing, purpose, or growth.

He's not unaware of how hard this, but nothing is too hard for God.

You Are a *JoyKeeper*

TRUTH: God is God, and you are not.

- Read Job 42:2; Jeremiah 32:17; Matthew 26:50–54.
- Prayer is powerful, and God hears every word. Take a few moments and pray for that person or situation.

#prayerstarter

Father, I have my sword out ready to go, and I sense you asking me to put it away. I have to admit this makes me feel helpless, but I also confess that every time I take out my sword and wave it about, it doesn't make things better. Give me the courage I need to let you take the lead. In Jesus's name, amen.

Day 14: Fill Me Up, Lord

I am the Lord your God, who brought you up out of the land of Egypt. Open your mouth wide and I will fill it.—Psalm 81:10

In Psalm 81, the psalmist refers to a group of people who didn't know which way to go. God had rescued them, but things weren't working out like they thought they should. They were out of slavery but acted as if they weren't free. They filled their days with things that led them further away from God's goodness rather than closer.

God, in his goodness, reminded them that he was there.

Don't try to fill your empty places with more activity.

Don't try to make yourself feel better temporarily.

Don't choose things that take you in the opposite direction of my love.

Choose me.

No one can fill us like God can.

Being busy isn't a problem, unless we use that busyness as an escape hatch.

Running after good things isn't a problem, unless we want those things to fill a need reserved for him.

Close out all the clutter and ask him to fill you back up. Do this before you take on more tasks. Do this before you make one more decision.

He alone has what you need and will fill you up.

You Are a *JoyKeeper*

TRUTH: God is God, and you are not.

- Read Psalm 81:16; 107:9; Isaiah 44:3; John 4:13–14.
- We put things that matter to us on the calendar, so mark a time on the calendar for just you and God. Consider it sacred, whether it's a few minutes or a longer time away to refuel.

#prayerstarter

Lord, I need what you have offered me as your daughter. Fill me. Not just a little, but let your presence and power and love overflow in the barren places. I've been spinning plates when what I need most has been there all along. Thank you for this time with you today. I love you. In Jesus's name, amen.

Day 15: Your One Thing

For in him we live and move and have our being.—Acts 17:28

I don't usually struggle with anxiety, but there it was. Concerned thoughts bubbled just under the surface. Questions pelted like gravel under the body of an old farm truck.

Am I doing enough?

Should I be doing more?

Am I doing this right?

Thoughts like these can hit any of us at any time. They surface in a marriage or close relationship. In a job or a ministry position or as we take a big step of faith.

There's a natural rhythm to anxious thoughts. They logically want to take us toward angst.

Luke describes a different rhythm in Acts 17:28. He says that we are free to live and move in Christ.

To move *in* him is to move with him.

This beautiful imagery acknowledges that God's Spirit is in us. Right there. Even in the midst of those anxious thoughts. He's aware of your doubts and questions, just as he's aware of the good stuff. When you feel anxious thoughts rising, he asks that you listen for him. He will lead toward peace, rather than away. He'll remind you of all the times you've walked through hard places before, and how he met you there.

One of the most powerful reminders is that God is God, and you are not. You can rest in this truth. The pressure to perform eases. The pressure to fix, strive, juggle, or make things happen in your timing is reordered to fit his rhythm rather than your own.

We *live* in rhythm with him.

We *move* in rhythm with him.

We *are* in rhythm with him.

You Are a *JoyKeeper*

TRUTH: God is God, and you are not.

- Read Acts 17:27–28; Job 12:10; Isaiah 8:17.
- Listen to your favorite worship song. Close your eyes and listen for the underlying rhythm. Isn't it beautiful? There's also a rhythm in your relationship with him.
- Ask God to meet you in the midst of that anxious thought.
- Join in rhythm with him.

#prayerstarter

Lord, worry doesn't change anything, but it does steal away my well-being. It takes my eyes off the good things right in front of me. Show me the rhythm of your thoughts in this matter. Lead me from worry to trust. Lead me from anxious thoughts to joyfully recalling all the times you've healed, turned around a difficult situation, or walked closely with me in the hard places—and how I came out stronger as a result. Let me move in rhythm with you. In Jesus's name, amen.

Day 16: When the Rains Come

Now that we know what we have—Jesus, this great High Priest with ready access to God—let's not let it slip through our fingers. We don't have a priest who is out of touch with our reality. He's been through weakness and testing, experienced it all—all but the sin. So let's walk right up to him and get what he is so ready to give. Take the mercy, accept the help.—Hebrews 4:14–18 MESSAGE

I half ran, half walked down the trail. My breath came in short spurts. My daily three-mile walk seemed like a lovely idea until the heavens opened and rain poured. The rain wasn't a big deal. I didn't mind that I was soaked. It was the rolling dark clouds and flashing lightning that made me feel exposed.

Was I supposed to stay out in the open, or hide under the branches of one of the large trees around me? Both seemed like a bad option. So I kept running until I finally made it home.

None of us like feeling exposed.

There have been times I've felt exposed in other ways. Illness strikes. The bank account is way too low. A close relationship hits a rough patch.

Have you been there? Are you there now?

In Hebrews 4, the author links God's rest to shelter. This is no ordinary shelter. It's as vast as the rest God entered after creating the world. The rains still come. Skies still split open. The earth shakes. Yet we find rest for our soul and our spirit. Not only that, but we come out on the other side of the storm stronger.

God is grieved when his people reject his rest. Throughout Scripture God called to his people.

Rest in me.

Stop trying to do this on your own.

I'm right here.

I have something better for you, if you'd only come to me.

The beautiful message in Hebrews 4 is that a safe place is not dependent on our own works. We yield to the truth that his rest becomes our refuge.

It's there, smack in the heart of his love for you.

You Are a *JoyKeeper*

TRUTH: God is your safe place.

- Read Psalm 119:28; Matthew 11:28–29; Hebrews 4:9–10.
- What is making you feel exposed (out in the open, bare, uncovered)?
- When you accept his offer of rest, the result is a safe place to land.
- Will you do that right now?

#prayerstarter

How many times have I tried to do things on my own, leaving you at a distance? Lord, you offer rest. This rest is as deep as the ocean and as wide as the universe. You won't force it on me, but you wait for me to see how much I need it. I confess that I am weary of standing in the rain alone. I'm running to your love and fully receive the rest you have for me. In Jesus's name, amen.

Day 17 : Rock and Refuge

When I am filled with cares, your comfort brings me joy.—
Psalm 94:19 CSB

When a person hurts us, most of us want to take revenge in our own hands. Our fear might be that someone will get away with wrongdoing if we don't address it ourselves. That's understandable.

While it's not something we take pleasure in talking about, there are people in the world who practice evil. They do unjust and unfair things to others, and it seemingly profits them.

This is what we find in Psalm 94 as the psalmist describes how the evil trample over the innocent. He cries out to God for justice.

This is a perfect case for revenge, but that's not what he asks of God. He asks him to be the *avenger* of wrongdoings and the people who committed them.

There is a difference between revenge and trusting God to avenge an evil deed.

We aren't asked to ignore what happened, but we are asked to not personally take on the task of payback or retaliation.

Revenge is a bitter road. It inflicts just as much, or more, damage on those who travel that road as it does on the transgressor. When we ask God to be the avenger, we may have a part to play (like seeking justice), but the emotional burden wrapped around the heart is released.

The psalmist described it like this:

> Blessed is the man whom You instruct, O Lord, and teach out of Your law, that You may give him rest from the days of adversity, until the pit is dug for the wicked.—Psalm 94:12–13 NKJV

This type of rest is a rock and a refuge. His mercy holds us up. We find comfort. We refuse to live a life dictated and defined by revenge, and that is a victory. While we are aware of our limitations, we are also aware of how great our God is—and that holds us firm and produces joy.

You Are a *Joy Keeper*

TRUTH: God is your safe place.

- Read Psalm 94:22; Proverbs 20:22; Romans 12:17–21.
- Seventeenth century cleric Jeremy Taylor said, "Revenge . . . is like a rolling stone, which, when a man hath forced up a hill, will return upon him with a greater violence, and break those bones whose sinews gave it motion."[1] What is one thing that happens when we hold on to revenge?
- Describe one thing that happens when a person lets go of revenge.
- What might it look like to allow God to be the avenger?

#prayerstarter

You are not asking me to allow evil to run rampant, or to pretend that evil didn't happen. You are asking me to release my need for revenge and to place that mountainous burden in your hands. So I say yes and thank-you. I'm tired of carrying it around. In Jesus's name, amen.

1. Jeremy Taylor, *The Beauties of J. Taylor: Selected from His Works with an Essay on His Life and Writings* (Glasgow: Blackie & Son, 1834), 45, https://books.google.com/books?id=kwEPAAAAIAAJ.

Day 18: There's a Difference

A vegetarian meal served with love is better than a big, thick steak with a plateful of animosity.—Proverbs 15:17 ISV

When I look up the definition of the word *critical*, it's a little bleak.

condemning

disparaging

disapproving

If you've been on the receiving end of unhelpful criticism, it may make you feel . . .

condemned

nitpicked

not enough

Constant or chronic criticism is miles away from helpful critique. The first highlights all the vulnerable parts of who you are and completely overlooks the good. It's dished out by a critical person. It may even be someone you love.

The words poke. They prod.

Helpful critique recognizes all the valuable parts of who you are or what you did while gently revealing areas where you can improve.

This builds you up. It helps you grow!

Scripture tells us that we are a *good* work. We were created for a purpose. We were formed in the image of God. When we embrace the words of a critical person as our identity, we are giving away a good thing.

Our identity is not that person's to take.

The chronic, unhelpful criticism is not ours to receive.

So we give ourselves permission to differentiate between a critical word and a helpful one.

We realize that words matter but God's words matter more.

Confront chronic criticism by pouring God's words over your heart daily. His words are a shield, a light, and help you to distinguish between a truth and a lie.

While you are at it, be kind to yourself.

Refuse to repeat the words of a broken person over your own heart, for you are a beautiful work of a good, good God.

You Are a Joykeeper

TRUTH: God is your safe place.

- Read Genesis 1:27; Isaiah 54:17; Zephaniah 3:17; Philippians 2:13.
- Write three words a critical person has spoken over you. Put a big X through those words.
- Write three words that God speaks over you in their place.

#prayerstarter

Lord, I may not be able to stop the hurtful words that fall from the lips of another, but I don't have to hold on to them as if they are true. Expose all the words I've tucked away in my heart that don't belong there. In Jesus's name, amen.

Day 19: What Is Honor?

Honor your father and mother.—Ephesians 6:2

She drove to her parents' home on Sunday. As she did, she braced for her father's critical words. She might be there only a couple of hours, but her father made comments about her parenting skills, about her opinions, and about the smallest of things. One day her son asked a question, one she had asked herself many times.

"Why do you let him do that?"

This wasn't easy to answer. Maybe it was easier to let it slide rather than confront him. He had always been this way, so chances were he wasn't going to change anytime soon. Then there was the tricky part, the Scripture she had been taught years earlier.

Honor your father and mother.

Was allowing her father to speak this way honor?

Honor means to "give value to a relationship." This concept is woven throughout Scripture. We are asked to give value (honor) to the relationship we have with our parents, with those who are older, and with those in authority. Similarly, parents are encouraged to give value (honor) to the relationship they have with their children by not provoking that child to anger. Employers are instructed to give value to the relationship they have with their employees by treating them fairly.

When a relationship is unhealthy, it's important that we do three things:

1. Don't confuse abuse with honor.
2. Clarify what we need.
3. Clarify how we can honor this relationship.

She loved her dad but knew the abuse would continue if she didn't share her needs. She needed her dad to stop saying hurtful words. She needed him to stop demeaning her in front of her family—or anyone else.

Then she continued the heart work.

If she wanted honor, she would also give it. She prayed that the change would begin in her. She didn't want to live in resentment. She didn't want to be angry at her dad every time she was with him. She had a hard conversation with him. She told him she loved him, but also how his words made her feel. She promised to be honest with him rather than allow bitterness to build.

Change didn't come overnight, but it was a beginning. It also freed her. Whether her dad was willing to change or not, she was changing.

We can be outwardly honoring and inwardly resentful. That's miserable. Knowing what honor is and isn't is helpful. Asking for honor is a strong move.

Desiring to give it in return is healing.

You Are a *JoyKeeper*

TRUTH: God is your safe place.

- Read Genesis 2:24; Proverbs 15:1; Matthew 10:13; Ephesians 6:2–4.
- What do you need from a critical person in your life?
- Are you willing to give these same things in return?
- What might that look like?

#prayerstarter

Father, I don't want to carry this anymore. If this abuse is hurting me or those I love, give me wisdom. Help me to forgive. If I'm stuck in old patterns, move me in a new direction. I pray you'll work on their heart, and I hold mine up too. In Jesus's name, amen.

Day 20: Who Has Our Ear?

Rehoboam rejected the advice the elders gave him and consulted the young men who had grown up with him and were serving him.—1 Kings 12:8

My head buzzed from the amount of advice received in one twenty-four-hour period. Social media and advertisements told me what to do, what to think, what to buy. I had just arrived home from a trip with a sweet relative. That person had enthusiastically informed me how fast I should go, where to turn, and what exit I should have taken, though I knew exactly where I was going.

With all of the noise in our ears, it can be hard to sort through good counsel versus bad.

In 1 Kings 12, Rehoboam is a young king and in need of wise counsel. He was chosen to succeed his father, Solomon. Though King Solomon was considered a great ruler, he had taxed his people heavily and required hard labor. The crowds were crying out for a gentler touch.

Rehoboam turned to a group of elders for guidance. They advised him to give the people what they asked. If he were a kinder king, the people would follow him gladly.

But a younger group of friends told Rehoboam to lay a heavier burden on the people and to be unmerciful.

He decided to take unwise counsel.

The people revolted. Nations divided. His legacy became a bitter rivalry that lasted to his dying day. All because he listened to, and acted on, unwise counsel.

There are numerous voices that arise when we need answers. When we don't know whom to listen to, we can ask:

Does this counsel lead to God's best for me or God's best in this situation?

Does the advisor love me enough to speak truth?

Does this person's life reflect the qualities I hope to have in my own life?

If the answer is no to *any* of these questions, that's a good reason to hit the pause button. We can be assured that there will always be people telling us what to do, but thankfully, we can listen to those who are wise and toss out the rest.

You Are a *JoyKeeper*

TRUTH: God is your safe place.

- Read 1 Kings 14:29–31; Psalm 51:6; James 3:17.
- If you are wrestling with what to do, go to God first. Then to wise counsel.
- If someone is giving you advice, ask the questions above.
- Are they wise counsel? Why or why not?

#prayerstarter

Lord, I will always come to you first, for you promise to listen. I also want to thank you for people who have wrestled with these things and who bring honesty and wisdom to the conversation. Help me to listen to what best reflects you. In Jesus's name, amen.

Day 21: Jesus-Plus Religion

It is for freedom that Christ has set us free. Stand firm, then, and do not let yourselves be burdened again by a yoke of slavery.—Galatians 5:1

A woman grew up in a faith community that taught Jesus-plus faith. From a young age, faith was about what she wore, how much she read the Bible, and how holy she lived. She couldn't live up to it no matter how hard she tried.

So she created stricter rules for herself, hoping it would help.

It didn't.

Jesus-plus religion is Jesus, *plus* all the extra stipulations piled on top by humans.

The Pharisees were well known for this. They added elaborate stipulations and additional laws. The rules were piled so high it was impossible to achieve.

In Galatians, Paul confronts Jesus-plus religion. Believers were growing in their faith and excited about what they were learning. Until a group of men whooshed in to throw old rules into the mix. They pointed fingers at the new believers, spewing warnings and telling how they were messing up. As they tried to resurrect the old laws that Jesus fulfilled on the cross, it was confusing and created a culture of shame.

While Paul was once the greatest of sinners, the *only* thing that rescued him was the love of Christ. Not rules. Not trying to please people.

He was justified by faith in Christ. Exonerated. Vindicated. Pardoned. Cleared. Freed!

It is for freedom that we have been set free.

This is the message Paul preached.

172

This is the message Jesus formed and fashioned when he came to rescue us. When we receive that freedom, we leave behind Jesus-plus religion. We are free to confess our mistakes and grow through them. We are free to admit when we're wrong and humbly ask for forgiveness.

We're free to accept his love and a fresh new beginning.

We're free to live as a reflection of his grace as we mature in our faith and walk with Jesus every single day.

This is where the real makeover of our heart and faith originates.

You Are a JoyKeeper

TRUTH: God's goodness is greater.

- Read Galatians 1:6–8; 5:6–8, 18.
- What is one problem that comes from adding our own twist to the gospel?
- What is one way to stay grounded in the truth?

#prayerstarter

Lord, show me any manmade rules I've added to my faith. Strip those away. Start your work on the inside. Do what only you can do. I love you. In Jesus's name, amen.

Day 22: When You Are Tempted

Let us hold resolutely to the hope we profess, for He who promised is faithful.—Hebrews 10:23 BSB

The Bible says you are a new person, and you believe it. You've been showing up. You are changing. You've said you are sorry and mean it, and your life reflects that. That doesn't mean you don't face temptation.

Your old life, which nearly destroyed you, tries to paint a shiny picture of your past. It tries to tell you that you lost something. You wonder if temptation is a sin.

No, you are in the trenches of your faith. Jesus rescued you and put your feet on a beautiful new path. There's nothing that makes our enemy more frustrated than that.

He's going to tempt you.

When tempted, look back to see how far God has brought you. Throw a party between you and God as you celebrate every victory. When tempted, ask the Holy Spirit to strip away the veil that makes those old things look shiny. Be honest with yourself of the cost they exacted from you and those you love. When tempted, check in with God often. He sees where you are going and how hard you are working.

You are running the race and that makes you brave.

When tempted, don't mistake difficulty for failure.

If we follow Jesus, we march into those more difficult places because that's where the miracles occur.

Maybe it's a miracle the whole world sees. Maybe only you and God see it.

It's still a miracle.

When tempted, feed your faith. Gather with good friends who love Jesus. Read books that teach and inspire. Journal, with your Bible open, as you soak in the Word.

As you do, remember this: God isn't measuring your walk of faith by your standards, or by those of anyone else. He sees your heart and your desire to follow him.

You are stronger than you know.

More courageous than you realize.

He will complete the work he began in you.

You Are a *JoyKeeper*

TRUTH: God's goodness is greater.

- Read Acts 4:13; 1 Corinthians 10:13; Hebrews 10:19–23; 12:1–3.
- It may not tempt others, but if it's a temptation to you, turn from it.
- Don't entertain it. Don't give it room.
- As you turn *from* temptation, focus on turning *to* Christ.

#prayerstarter

Lord, that old thing robbed me. It took and took from me and those I love. When it seems shiny and alluring, help me to see it for what it really is. Remind me that your plan for me is good. When I am on that hard path, help me rejoice in the miracle under way. In Jesus's name, amen.

Day 23 : Do Not Trespass

But God, who is rich in mercy, because of His great love with which
He loved us, even when we were dead in trespasses, made us alive
together with Christ (by grace you have been saved), and raised us
up together, and made us sit together in the heavenly places in Christ
Jesus, that in the ages to come He might show the exceeding riches
of His grace in His kindness toward us in Christ Jesus.—Ephesians
2:4–7 NKJV

When we come across a large sign with the words "Do not trespass," what do we do? We normally turn around. That sign may indicate a private driveway off limits to the public. It may be a warning not to venture down a treacherous road.

When Paul talks about trespasses, he is referring to a line crossed.

We intentionally ignore a spiritual boundary and move into territory that is not God's best for us. When that happens, we may hide out of shame. That secret becomes a stronghold. Shame is a coffin that tries to hold you with trespasses, sin, and secrets, but this is a powerful truth to remember: Jesus loved you while you were yet dead in your trespasses and sins.

He loves you even as the world tells you that you are unlovable.

He loves you even as you tell yourself you went too far, that it's too late.

He loves you even as shame whispers that God can't or won't forgive you.

When you cross that line, you aren't stuck there. You don't have to remain in that sin. You can turn around and run into the arms of your heavenly Father. When you confess that sin, he is faithful and just and he forgives and cleanses you from that sin.

It's a fresh slate.

He waits for you.

Bring it to the Light and start anew.

You Are a *JoyKeeper*

TRUTH: God's goodness is greater.

- Read Psalm 103:12; Isaiah 53:5; Luke 15:21–24; Romans 5:16–18, 20.
- We can get stuck in a secret. That secret can become our stronghold.
- Throw a light on that secret and rob it of its power.
- Tell God everything and ask for wisdom on your next step.

#prayerstarter

Jesus, I'm tired of this secret I've carried. It whispers that I am stuck. You love me while I am yet dead in my trespasses; how can that be? Yet I believe it is true, so I step into the Light. I give this secret to you. Help me to live a transparent and free life. In Jesus's name, amen.

Day 24: Something New

But forget all that— it is nothing compared to what I am going to do. For I am about to do something new. See, I have already begun! Do you not see it? I will make a pathway through the wilderness. I will create rivers in the dry wasteland.—Isaiah 43:18–19 NLT

The Israelites were captives, immigrants in a strange land. Hundreds of miles of wilderness lay between them and freedom. If they tried to find their way out, wasteland and lack of water would swallow them up.

For many, captivity was all they had known.

Worse, sin had led them to captivity.

Forget all that.

When the prophet Isaiah asked them to put the past behind them, his words were startling. God wanted to do something new, but in order for it to begin, they had to stop looking backward.

Only God could form a road in the wilderness.

Only God was capable of creating a roaring river in the wasteland.

They couldn't see it yet, but the promise was there.

When God restores our sinful heart, he wants to do a new work. It's tempting to look back and point out how bad we once were.

Do you know how far I ran from you?

God wants to do something new in you.

I'm so afraid I'll mess up again.

God wants to do something new in you.

Our heavenly Father is aware of what led you to captivity. He asks that you believe there's a future for you. He carves out a road where there seems to be none and asks that you follow it.

He points to himself as your Source and asks that you trust him.

If you've lived in captivity and exile due to sin, it's hard to believe you can be anything else. That's a natural response. When you take your eyes off what is behind you, you are freed to anticipate the *new* God wants to do in you.

That's where the supernatural begins. You partner with him in the new.

You can't change what is behind, but you can trust that new is ahead, with his help.

You Are a *JoyKeeper*

TRUTH: God's goodness is greater.

- Read Isaiah 42:9; 43:18–19; Ezekiel 36:26; Romans 6:4.
- Write down one word that describes what you want to move past.
- Ask God for a new word to take its place. Write that word down and put it where you can see it every day.
- Read Isaiah 43:18–19 again. Place your name in the Scripture. Say it out loud.

#prayerstarter

I can't do this without you, and you don't ask me to. I'm thankful for the new that you are doing and what is to come. New in me. New in those I love. Help me to move beyond the past, to fully live in the possibilities of what can be. In the name of Jesus, amen.

Day 25: You're Found!

For the Son of Man came to seek and to save the lost.—Luke 19:10

I raced through the store with a stroller. Two children tucked in tight. One on the loose.

He had been by my side seconds earlier.

I turned around and he was gone. I called out to anyone who would listen. "Have you seen my son? He's about this high," I said, holding my hand just so.

Ten minutes later I found him. He hadn't even known he was lost, but this mama's world was right again. I was willing to push that oversized stroller to the ends of the earth until he was safe in my arms.

When Jesus found Zacchaeus in the branches of a sycamore tree, he was also looking for a lost son. Zacchaeus had drifted from his roots.

Jesus went out of his way, leaving the crowds to stand at the base of a sycamore tree. He called Zacchaeus out of that tree to go eat a meal together. That encounter changed Zacchaeus from that day forward. He had a change of heart and a change of direction.

When we are overcoming shame, we may feel a bit lost.

Lost doesn't always mean we are physically missing. It can mean "directionless." We aren't sure where we are going or what is next. Thankfully, Jesus came to seek and save those who are lost. You may not know which direction to go next, but the one who found you does.

He's inviting you to walk with him in that healing place, even when it feels like you are standing still. This is not a reprimand, but restoration. He's willing to take the time needed to make you whole.

As you leave behind your old life to start a new page in your story, he'll show you what today holds, and then again tomorrow. You don't have to have the whole plan, because walking with him daily is the plan.

Everything else flows from that.

You've been found, my friend, and that changes you forever.

You Are a *JoyKeeper*

TRUTH: God's goodness is greater.

- Read Psalm 16:11; Isaiah 40:11; Ezekiel 34:12; Luke 19:1–10.
- Remember a time you lost something precious. Describe how you felt when you found it.
- Your heavenly Father feels the same way about you.

#prayerstarter

I've been lost and now I'm found. I can spend the rest of my life looking back at how lost I was, or I can rejoice that you never stopped looking for me. Thank you for that. In Jesus's name, amen.

Day 26: Let's Eat!

Jesus said to them, "Come and have breakfast." None of the disciples dared ask him, "Who are you?" They knew it was the Lord.—John 21:12

Have you ever caught a whiff of something cooking and it transported you back? The aroma of fresh-baked bread, hot cookies right out of the oven, or that tangy spice unique to your family or culture. It hits all your senses and brings memories with it.

I wonder if that's how Peter felt that day sitting around a campfire.

He and others began their day by the water.

Peter harbored a wounded soul, because the last time he saw Jesus, he let him down.

Then they saw someone on the shore.

"Caught any fish?" the man asked.

"No," they replied.

"Throw your net on the other side," the stranger said.

They followed his instructions and suddenly the net was full. This wasn't the first time this had happened. There was another time someone asked them to throw their nets in the water. The nets were so full they nearly burst.

Could it be?

It was!

When Peter recognized the reincarnated Jesus, he threw off his outer garment and plunged into the water, swimming furiously toward his Savior. The others followed in the boat, tugging heavy nets behind them.

Grab some of those fish. Let's have breakfast.

When Jesus invited Peter to eat with him, he knew what Peter was thinking. Peter had failed so badly, it might seem there was no room for him in Jesus's plan. Jesus reminded Peter there was still work to do.

Yes, Peter had made a mistake, but Jesus didn't make a mistake in choosing him.

Feed my sheep, Peter.

The aroma of those words filled Peter's wounded soul, just as the steaming fish filled his belly.

If you have made a mistake, your seat has not been taken from you. You are still part of the plan. Receive his healing words and start anew, for there's work to do.

You Are a *JoyKeeper*

TRUTH: God has a seat for you.

- Read Matthew 26:69–75; Luke 5:5–7; John 21:1–15.
- In John 21, there are two catches. One hundred fifty-three were captured in the net. The second was the fish cooking over the fire as Peter reached Jesus. Jesus met his discouraged friend with a fire, food, and fellowship.
- What does that say about our relationship with Jesus?

#prayerstarter

Jesus, there are beautiful big things you'll ask me to do. You'll ask me to trust you. You'll ask me to receive your grace. You'll ask me to throw my "net" over the side of the boat, even when I feel like I've failed or have nothing to show. You meet me there with provision, food for my soul, and fellowship. I'm so grateful for that. In Jesus's name, amen.

Day 27: Greater

*Most assuredly, I say to you, he who believes in Me, the works
that I do he will do also; and greater works than these he will do,
because I go to My Father. And whatever you ask in My name, that
I will do, that the Father may be glorified in the Son. If you ask
anything in My name, I will do it.*—John 14:12–14 NKJV

When we look at old photos, there can be a range of emotions. That hair! Those clothes. Why didn't anyone tell us that fashion trend was so awful?

When I look at old photos, I see a long-legged, coltish teenager with a big smile. She newly called herself a believer. She didn't know she could be a world-changer. She didn't have a rich spiritual heritage to hold up as a legacy. She didn't have credentials.

If you were to tell her there was a seat for her, she would struggle to believe you. She knew God loved her, and that was soul altering, but it didn't seem possible that she could be a world-changer. Not when she looked at what everyone else brought to the team.

If I could go back, I'd tell that lanky teenager that belief in Christ is what changes the world. Not one person alone. I'd tell her the church is filled with all kinds of people who stumble into the love of Christ. That it's rich with an assortment of giftings, backgrounds, experiences, ethnicities, cultures, faith stories, levels of spiritual maturity, and personalities.

I'd point out that, like a pot of roiling jambalaya, there are many ingredients. There's a pinch of brokenness and a gallon of healing. It's filled with work-in-progress people dealing with ego, pride, ambition, humility, and every other ingredient that comes with humanity.

Jesus knew that full well when he called us. In spite of that, he spoke these words: "I tell you the truth, anyone who believes in me will do the same works I have done, and even greater works, because I am going to be with the Father" (John 14:12 NLT).

Greater wasn't more spectacular. It was a longer, more vast reach as one by one we fanned out in his name and shared the gospel year after year, until his return. Our differences are exactly what he uses to accomplish that.

Your story relates to one. My story relates to another.

Your experience speaks into the heart of one. My story another.

Jesus chooses the weak and fragile things to reveal God's greatness.

And as we live in him, we do greater things.

You Are a Joy Keeper

TRUTH: God has a seat for you.

- Read Psalm 8:2; John 14:11–14; 1 Corinthians 1:27.
- Find an old photo of yourself. Create a timeline of how far faith has brought you since that picture was taken.
- Share one story from that timeline with someone else.

#prayerstarter

Jesus, it's easy to forget how far you've brought me. Thank you for every intervention, every miracle, every time you showed me something new. I love you so very much. In Jesus's name, amen.

Day 28: Awkward

Brothers and sisters, I do not consider myself yet to have taken hold of it. But one thing I do: Forgetting what is behind and straining toward what is ahead, I press on toward the goal to win the prize for which God has called me heavenward in Christ Jesus.—Philippians 3:13–14

I once knew a guy who grew five inches over the summer. That surge of growth caused him to develop a problem with his joints and knees called Osgood-Schlatter's disease. He was growing so quickly his bones were surpassing the development of his muscles and tendons.

He struggled with his new height. He didn't know what to do with his longer arms. He banged his head on door frames.

He felt awkward and clumsy because, well . . . he was.

Eventually he became comfortable with his long legs and long arms. He learned to gauge a door frame so he wouldn't hit his head. He bought clothes to fit the length of his arms and legs.

He was no longer just a tall guy. He lived as a tall guy.

We are invited to experience more than just an initial encounter with faith. Doors are opened in ministry, at work, in our families, or in our communities. He places people in our lives who don't know Jesus. He reveals broken places in the world where love is needed.

As you step into deeper faith, it may feel awkward.

It might not feel like a good fit. You are finding your way. Sometimes it feels like you take a huge step forward, only to lose that and more the next day.

What if we accepted awkward as part of the growth process?

- Instead of beating ourselves up, we keep going.
- Instead of looking at the finish line, we see every step along the way as key.
- Instead of pointing at anyone else, we acknowledge how far he's brought us.

We stop living as if we are short when Jesus sees us as tall.
We press on, keeping our eyes on him.
Even when it's awkward, we are still moving forward as long as we follow Jesus.

You Are a *JoyKeeper*

TRUTH: God has a seat for you.

- Read Ephesians 1:17–23; Philippians 3:13–14; James 1:5.
- When feelings of awkwardness hit, remind yourself that growth always involves awkward. Celebrate as you march into new arenas of faith.
- What do you feel God asking you to do?

#prayerstarter

Lord, if there is no awkward, there is little opportunity for growth. Today I choose to see this awkward moment as a diamond in the rough. I am being polished, refined, redeemed, restored. Thank you for the awkward in this season, and for the beauty that will come from it. In Jesus's name, amen.

Day 29 : What Do I Love?

God can do anything, you know—far more than you could ever
imagine or guess or request in your wildest dreams! He does it not
by pushing us around but by working within us, his Spirit deeply
and gently within us.—Ephesians 3:20 MESSAGE

I have a friend who loves purses. She switches between seasons
and outfits.

Personally, I've never owned more than a couple at a time.
I see them for their utility—something to hold my keys and gum.
She sees them as fashion and a part of her personality.

One day she was praying and asked this question:

God, I love you. How can you use what I naturally love to
help others?

She didn't have purses on her mind when she began that prayer.
Not one whit. But when she listed things she loved or loved to do,
purses were high on the list.

That felt silly. How could God use a love of purses?

Shortly after her prayer, she started collecting gently used purses
to sell online. She had no idea how people would respond, but she
found lots of other women who loved purses and they snapped
them up. She had an eye for quality and often discovered purses
at garage sales or at the local Goodwill for pennies on the dollar.
The profit margin was great!

She donated 100 percent of her profit to help rescue young
women trapped in slavery.

Who knew that a love of purses could make a difference?

God did.

When we stop to think about what we love, his name tops the
list. That makes sense, but what if we combine what we naturally

love as we partner with him? That might be writing. It might be physical fitness, hiking, or kayaking. Perhaps you naturally love children or teenagers or the elderly? Maybe you love DIY or have amazing organizational skills. Perhaps you love to lead, gather, connect. It could be that you have a bent for social justice.

Whatever it is, we stop waiting for God to hand deliver a special call that looks like anyone else's and instead step into ministry right where we love.

We believe the Holy Spirit can work through it and use it for good.

Today, ask one simple question. Make it a prayer.

Lord, I love you and I love [fill in the blank]. What can you do with these two things?

Because God can do anything, far more than we can imagine in our wildest dreams.

You Are a *JoyKeeper*

TRUTH: God has a seat for you.

- Read 2 Corinthians 9:7–8; Ephesians 3:20; 1 Peter 4:10.
- Answer the question "What do I love?" You might be surprised at the answer.
- Don't limit your answer to the ordinary. See where it takes you.

#prayerstarter

Father, I think I limit you. I look around and see what people are doing, and I think that's the model. You are more creative than that. As I hold up what I naturally love, show me a way to use it to love others in your name. Amen.

Day 30: Joy-Wrapped

But the Holy Spirit produces this kind of fruit in our lives: love, joy, peace, patience, kindness, goodness, faithfulness, gentleness, and self-control. There is no law against these things!—Galatians 5:22–23 NLT

When I read the list of attributes in Galatians 5, I want to be all of those things.

I long to love like Jesus.

I desire to be marked by joy.

It's my hope to bring peace where I go, and to be patient with people and with God's timing. I'd love for people to remember me as gentle, faithful, and good. Self-control is something I work at, because I need it.

The truth is I am not all of these things all of the time.

Galatians 5:22–23 is not a list of you-must-dos, but an inventory of equipment. All of this is available to us. It's inside of us because the Holy Spirit dwells in us. These are his attributes, not ours. As we intentionally choose to listen to his voice and follow it, at some point these traits are reflected in us as well.

We live as Spirit-led believers.

We love because love is the greatest fruit—for everything else flows from it.

We understand that rock-solid joy is tied to our relationship with God, so that's where we turn.

We seek peace that passes understanding as we stand on a foundation that cannot be shaken.

Patience, kindness, goodness, faithfulness, self-control—we know these are not decisions of a spur-of-the-moment heart, but produced by seeds planted in deep soil day by day as we make faith our way of life. They push through the soil, tiny and tender until they become strong.

As we do, the Holy Spirit draws us to the One who loves us best. And our Spirit-led heart becomes a joy-wrapped heart.

You Are a *JoyKeeper*

TRUTH: God has a seat for you.

- Read John 14:26; Romans 8:14–17; Galatians 5:22–23.
- The Holy Spirit is in you, and so is your natural flesh. Feed one more than the other. Trust one over the other.
- When you feel ill-equipped, remember you have everything you need. Ask for it.

#prayerstarter

Holy Spirit, you are inside of me, and that's hard to fathom. I realize I cannot be all of these things on my own, and God doesn't ask it of me. When I reach for what is natural, remind me of the supernatural so very close at hand. In Jesus's name, amen.

study guide for groups

L eading a study is life-changing. Not just for the women in your group, but also for you. I have led studies in my own home for years.

May I share a few things I learned along the way?

Before the event

- Pick a date, time, and place for your gathering.
- Invite friends, family, or coworkers.
- Confirm whether they would like you to order their book and let them know the cost.
- Order the number of books you will need.

On the day or night of your study

- Remember that most women aren't looking for fancy. They want community and connection.
- Welcome each woman individually (I usually ask a friend to help with this).
- Place a sticky note on each book with the participant's name.

- Consider tying a simple ribbon around the book or placing a book mark in each copy.
- Don't worry about cleaning your home from top to bottom. Inviting others into our spaces encourages them to do the same.
- Serve a light refreshment. Keep it simple. Cookies are always welcome.
- Get to know one another. Do simple introductions and get acquainted. Play a name game to create laughter and put everyone at ease.
- Before your gathering, read the introduction. Highlight parts that get you excited and share them with the group. On the first night, share why you chose this book. Vulnerability is a beautiful gift. It invites others to do the same.
- Invite women to be circle-breakers and bring friends.
- Invite each woman to share (some won't want to, and that's okay).

How to Study *JoyKeeper*

You know your group better than anyone, so these are suggestions only.

JoyKeeper is an interactive book that is helpful for personal study but also powerful for group study. Each chapter includes questions and pause points throughout, as well as a reflection portion at the end.

Invite women to work through each chapter on their own. One chapter per week equals a six-week study, which is usually doable.

At the beginning of your gathering, start with prayer.

Ask women to share aha moments or times they wrestled as they read a chapter. Share your own thoughts from time to time, especially if there was a portion where you and God connected.

Don't be afraid to stop and pray or encourage (without giving advice). This is often where community makes a difference.

Gathering women may feel intimidating at first, but you are making a difference, more than you know.

In addition to the pause points and questions in each chapter, I created discussion questions to help get the conversation flowing. (See the following pages.)

Hey friends, one thing I love to do is to pop in to a study group. If you are leading a study, whether in your home, at a church, or in an organization, contact me through www.suzanneeller.com, and let's see if we can find a date when I can drop in and pray over your beautiful community.

—*Suzie*

group discussion questions

Introduction and Chapter 1

Suzie says, "A JoyKeeper is someone who experiences real life. She feels all the feelings. She isn't afraid to be honest when things are hard. She's tethered to something bigger than her feelings. I know this because I wrote this book in an extended season of sorrow" (page 14).

Describe a time you experienced sorrow.

What is one emotion you experienced?

How is God a safe place for those emotions?

Was there a verse you held on to during that season?

Chapter 2

What do you think about this quote found in chapter 2 (page 36)?

An unhealed person can find offense in pretty much anything anyone does. A healed person understands the actions of others have nothing to do with them. Each day you get to decide which you will be.—Unknown

Share a recent moment when you had to make this type of choice.

What was one way to respond as a healed woman?

What might be an unhealthy way to respond?

In what ways does responding as a healed woman change the event or you?

Chapter 3

Suzie says, "When we put down assignments that aren't ours, we are released to do the assignments that are" (page 60).

What is your reaction to this statement, and why?

What might chalk-line faith look like in this season for you?

Name a fear you have about putting down that assignment.

(This is a perfect time to pray. We are stronger together!)

Chapter 4

There are many different personality tests, and you may have taken a few of them. Often, they expose something new about us. They also help us to learn about the way our friends or family are wired, and that has the potential to strengthen our relationships.

Describe a test you've taken and what you learned.

Of course, there is no truth greater than Scripture. Psalm 139 says we are uniquely and miraculously created. Imagine God's joy as each distinctive person is tenderly placed in his or her mother's womb.

What might happen if we truly believed this about ourselves?

Chapter 5

Let's do a poll. Which of the following statements do you believe is true? (Read both statements aloud and ask for a showing of hands.)

Shame is a result of other people's words over our hearts.

Shame comes from the words we speak over our own hearts.

When Suzie was writing the book, she shared this same poll with friends. The results surprised her.

Thirty-three percent said it was others' words that produced ongoing shame. Sixty-seven percent said it was their own words that made them feel shame—and those words were rarely out loud, but internal.

How can we shift the conversation in our own hearts?

Is there a difference between shame and conviction, and why is it important to know the difference?

Chapter 6

When we talk about taking a seat, we might limit it to taking a physical seat. A place in a ministry or job. Maybe we define that as a specific role.

That's not what this chapter is talking about. It's believing that we are part of God's plan. It's believing that he knows us and invites us to join in his mission.

Suzie says, "It's not what you do that delights God. It's who you are" (page 114). What does that mean?

Community is messy. Describe how community has changed or helped you, even in the messiness.

Describe one way we can help each other find a seat—even in this community.

acknowledgments

I t seems impossible that this is book number 11, but none of them were birthed in isolation. This was no different. A team of family and friends stood shoulder-to-shoulder with me through every word.

I'm grateful for my husband, Richard.

Babe, you are my greatest cheerleader. You took care of the house and making dinner in the end stretch of writing this book. You wrapped around me when we were hit with such hard news. I'm grateful how much you love what I do.

Thank you to my children and my littles, who love me well. I want to give a special thank you to my son, Ryan.

Son, when I first wrote a part of your story, you asked me to go deeper. This was with your permission (and your and Kristin's encouragement). You called often through the writing process. You listened as I wrestled through chapter 5. You are living transparently in your story and showing what grace looks like. Thank you for that.

Jeff Braun of Bethany House Publishers stepped in as my new editor with this book.

Jeff, your kindness was evident from day one.

I love the Bethany House team. Every last one of you.

I am also grateful for Whitney Gossett, of The Fedd Agency, who championed this book and this author.

Thank you to Maggie, Stephanie, Jammie, Brandi, Desiree, Terry, Kim, Tamela, Jem, and Tyanne. These beautiful women were my focus group while writing *JoyKeeper*.

Thank you, ladies. I loved the honesty of our conversations.

Last, I'm beyond thankful for *you*, the reader. Many of you have walked with me as a friend through several books now. I've met some of you in person and my life is richer because of it.

Suzanne (Suzie) Eller is a bestselling author, Bible teacher, and podcaster. Suzie served with Proverbs 31 Ministries for fourteen years as a writer and speaker. She has been featured on numerous media outlets such as Focus on the Family, *100 Huntley Street*, *Aspiring Women*, K-LOVE, DayStar, and many others.

Suzie is the co-host of the *More Than Small Talk* podcast, along with Holley Gerth and Jennifer Watson. This popular podcast reaches women across the world. It's a part of the KLRC podcast network. To tune in, find it on your favorite podcast app or stream it at www.klrc.com/podcasts/more-than-small-talk.

Suzie has been married to Richard for forty years and is a mom to three grown children and their spouses. She's in love with six littles who call her Gaga. Suzie's favorite things to do are hiking and kayaking, or dancing to the music at the farmer's market with her littles.

Connect with Suzie

Find all kinds of fun freebies and more
at her website: www.suzanneeller.com

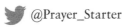 @SuzanneEller and @MoreThanSmallTalk

 @Prayer_Starter

@suzanneeller

IF YOU APPRECIATED

JoyKeeper

When you leave a review on Amazon or any other site, it makes such a difference. It helps another woman to hear your words. It encourages this author more than you can imagine. Thank you for leaving a review or telling someone else about *JoyKeeper*.

More from Suzanne Eller

Full of warmth and vulnerability, Suzanne Eller unpacks the promises Jesus shared with His disciples about the Holy Spirit, showing you how to stop settling for good enough and start truly living by His power. When you learn to unwrap the gift of His presence, you'll find the world-changing, soul-stirring life of passion and purpose God is waiting to give you.

The Spirit-Led Heart

In her sincere and conversational way, bestselling author Suzanne Eller shows that when you take a step away from the uncertainty, to-do lists, worries, and excuses, you take a step toward the One who promises to delight and surprise by transforming who you are, how you live, and how you impact the world. *Because where you are going is not as important as Who you go with.*

Come With Me

What if Jesus walked up to you right now and invited you to follow him—no questions asked? When the original disciples said yes, they had no idea what that meant. But they had Jesus to walk alongside them— and so do you! Join Suzanne on this thought-provoking, yearlong adventure through Luke, and discover the beauty of following where he leads.

Come With Me Devotional